Narrative of Sojourner Truth

Narrative of

SOJOURNER TRUTH

Edited and with an Introduction by

MARGARET WASHINGTON

Vintage Classics

Vintage Books

A Division of Random House, Inc., New York

A Vintage Classics Original, February 1993
First Edition

Introduction, Notes, Note on the Editions, and Bibliography
Copyright © 1993 by Margaret Washington

Library of Congress Cataloging-in-Publication Data
Washington, Margaret.
Narrative of Sojourner Truth / edited and with an introduction
by Margaret Washington.—1st ed.
p.   cm.—(Vintage classics)
Includes bibliographical references and index.
ISBN 0-679-74035-X
1. Truth, Sojourner, d. 1883. 2. Afro-Americans—Biography.
3. Abolitionists—United States—Biography. 4. Social reformers—
United States—Biography. I. Title. II. Series.
E185.97.T8W36   1993
305.567'092—dc20
[B]   92-56355
CIP

Book design by Rebecca Aidlin

Manufactured in the United States of America
10 9 8 7 6 5 4

Contents

I told Jesus it would be all right,

If he changed my name.

—AFRICAN-AMERICAN SPIRITUAL

Introduction

THE ENDURING LEGACY OF SOJOURNER TRUTH

❁

SOJOURNER TRUTH was the most notable and highly regarded African-American woman in the nineteenth century. She was devoted to the antislavery movement and was a fiery advocate of women's rights. She practiced spiritualism, temperance, hydrotherapy, perfectionism, and Grahamism. She was a mystic and a witty, folksy storyteller whose narrations always contained a compelling message. Towering in both stature and oral eloquence, Sojourner Truth was an omnipresent, quintessential figure among the progressive forces that refashioned nineteenth-century America.

Many doors were closed to African-American women in her day, but it was difficult to shut out Sojourner Truth. She was bold and insistent. Her teaching, preaching, and speaking methods; her moving renditions of Methodist hymns and songs of her own creation; her intuitive, universal insights; her unfailing commitment to black progress; and her enduring friendships with erudite American reformers made Sojourner a force in history. She even held audiences with two American presidents in behalf of her people. Scholars, dramatists, schoolchildren, and others in popular circles still recite her speeches, recall her maxims, and praise her contributions.

In her lifetime, Sojourner Truth was among the most quoted

activists. Her penetrating one-line comments captured the heart of moral, social, political, and religious issues. For example, when the 1850 Fugitive Slave Law tested antislavery activists' commitment to moral suasion and nonviolence, black abolitionist Frederick Douglass, along with many others, was angry and disillusioned. At a highly charged abolitionist rally, Douglass spoke out in his customary "flight of eloquence," articulating the mood of the militant wing. "The Negro," he said, must rise from degradation through their own efforts. Strike off the black man's shackles, said Douglass, "and he will rise by the power of his native intelligence and his own strong right arm." "Be careful Frederick," cautioned the pacifist Sojourner. "Is God Almighty dead!?" Her words were "perfectly electrical, and thrilled through the whole house, changing as by a flash the whole feeling of the audience." Douglass quickly modified his meaning.[1]

Among black abolitionists, Sojourner Truth formed lasting friendships with African Methodist Bishop Daniel Payne. She spoke at his church and at Wilberforce University, which he helped found. Sojourner's younger, more militant associate, Mary Shadd Cary, was editor of the Canada-based *Provincial Freeman*. Cary enjoyed quoting Sojourner when giving her own incendiary speeches.

Frederick Douglass first met Sojourner Truth in 1844 at the Northampton utopian community where he was sometimes a guest. The self-taught Douglass condescendingly recollected Sojourner as "a genuine specimen of the uncultured negro" who "seemed to please herself and others best when she put her ideas in the oddest forms." Douglass was both put off and enchanted by this uneducated woman who considered herself his equal in discourse and intelligence, if not in literacy and posturing. She was, he wrote, a "strange compound of wit and wisdom, of wild enthusiasm, and flint-like common sense, who seemed to feel it her duty to trip me up in my speeches and ridicule my efforts to speak and act like a person of cultivation and refinement."[2]

Along with Sojourner Truth's popularity in antebellum reform circles came notoriety among proslavery people, the majority of Americans before the Civil War. As the debate over slavery raged, Sojourner was sometimes harassed. Western states were particularly virulent toward abolitionists. On one occasion, Sojourner was told that the building she was to speak in would be burned if she attempted her address. "Then I will speak to the ashes," she replied. In another instance she was mauled so badly in a mob attack that she walked with a cane for the rest of her life. But Sojourner Truth stayed in the fray, believing that God would protect her and that her message warranted the danger involved in its deliverance.[3]

Sojourner Truth's national acceptance and popularity outside progressive circles were greatly enhanced in 1863. The year began with the January 1 signing of the Emancipation Proclamation and America's acceptance that the Civil War was no longer "a white man's war" over states' rights. That was also the year that Harriet Beecher Stowe published an account of her 1853 meeting with Sojourner, entitled "The Libyan Sibyl," in *Atlantic Monthly*. The article enhanced Sojourner's reputation, since *Uncle Tom's Cabin* had made Stowe one of America's most popular writers. In the account, Stowe took the liberty of distorting and lyricizing their meeting. But the immediate impression of Sojourner that she advanced was candid and memorable.

Stowe seemed genuinely impressed, and perhaps discomfited, by this sinewy African-American woman in Quaker dress. She noted Sojourner's imperious carriage, extreme height, and large, sparkling eyes. "I do not recollect ever to have been conversant with anyone who had more of that silent and subtle power which we call personal presence than this woman," wrote Stowe. She added that the "self-possessed" Sojourner was perfectly "at her ease," displaying "an unconscious superiority" mixed with humor as she looked down upon the renowned author.[4]

Stowe's article was published amid rumors that Sojourner Truth was dead; hence, it was meant partly as an obituary. Although she was ill after having been badly roughed up and arrested in Indiana by proslavery forces, Sojourner was very much alive. And the national calamity that had led to emancipation actually gave new significance to her life. The aging but indefatigable sage seemed to be everywhere, displaying her well-spring of devotion, biting satire, humor, and gaiety. Sojourner recruited "colored troops" for a Michigan regiment; worked as "counselor to the freedpeople" in Arlington Heights, Virginia; met with Harriet Tubman, who had been on the front lines with black soldiers in South Carolina; and conversed with Abraham Lincoln. Perhaps her crowning achievement of the war years was desegregating the Washington, D.C., streetcars. The conductors' refusal to allow her to ride led to a successful lawsuit. It was a victory which cost Sojourner a dislocated shoulder; nevertheless, she was among the first freedom riders.[5]

Immediately after the Civil War, Sojourner aided freedpeople desiring to leave the crowded hovels and makeshift shelters of Washington, D.C., and Arlington Heights. Some were relocated in Michigan while others went to upstate New York, although the endeavor was only moderately successful. From 1865 until her death in 1883, Sojourner Truth doubled her efforts on behalf of African-Americans despite her age and infirmities. Disillusioned by black poverty, white racism, and violence, she encouraged the government to make land available to black Southerners. Her advocacy of woman suffrage and other postwar crusades was secondary to this commitment. Many African-American leaders, like Frederick Douglass, expressed undogged faith in the failed political process. Others, like Henry Highland Garnet, became expatriates. Sojourner's "tongue of fire" not only proclaimed black America's birthright, while challenging the nation to incorporate African-Americans in its vision of economic progress, but also upheld the right of blacks to live with dignity separately.[6]

Sojourner Truth probably intended to become a traveling preacher when she began her trek in 1843. Indeed, there was already a tradition of black women itinerants. Listeners throughout Connecticut and Massachusetts were as mesmerized by her firsthand account of bondage as by her preaching and singing. She never tired of representing the collective memory and vision of black America. In the 1840s Sojourner spoke at antislavery rallies in New England. In 1850, following publication of the *Narrative,* she operated out of Salem, Ohio, using the office of the *Anti-Slavery Bugle* as headquarters. She traveled by buggy, on foot, by boat and rail—sometimes alone, sometimes in the company of other abolitionists. Always, she carried a parcel full of her little books. "I sell the shadow to support the substance" was her engaging motto. In 1857, as her travels took her repeatedly to the west, she relocated permanently to Battle Creek, Michigan.[7]

As her range of progressive causes expanded, Sojourner Truth met and bonded with many people. She moved easily and comfortably in Hicksite Quaker circles (an outcast antislavery wing of the sect which had helped her recover her son in Ulster County), added Quakerism to her ecumenical philosophy, and adopted Quaker attire. Women's rights advocates, abolitionists, and spiritualists were some of Sojourner's most constant supporters. Members of the prominent Titus and Merritt families of Battle Creek were her warmest companions. Minnie Merritt Fay remembered Sojourner as a welcome guest whose presence at the dinner table "was often criticized" by some of the city's influential residents:

When she returned from Trips to Washington and Kansas, she related her experiences to the group of friends around the table. . . . I can see her seated there, tall and straighter than anyone else. Her face always beaming and earnest while relating her experiences. . . . We loved to hear her talk. Her wonderful voice was deep and smooth.[8]

Sojourner Truth was an inspiration for ordinary African-Americans, particularly women. In her answer to a letter from Sojourner, one young New York woman's unabashed race pride reveals how important a symbol Sojourner was and offers a glimpse of early black nationalism:

This is the second epistle I have addressed to you. . . .
    You asked me if I was of your race. I am proud to say I am of the same race that you are, I am coloured thank God for that; I have not the curse of God upon me for enslaving human beings, did I say I was proud yes thrice proud of my race. . . . Although crushed and enslaved kept back and rejected their talents will shine and in some way they will show their superiority.[9]

Sojourner Truth's early life closely paralleled that of most nineteenth-century African-Americans. Named Isabella, she was born a slave in 1797, in Hurley, Ulster County, New York, the second youngest of twelve or thirteen children of James and Elizabeth. All were owned by Johannes Hardenbergh, Jr., an influential rural Dutch patroon, American patriot, and heir to the Hardenberg Patent, a massive but contested land grant which included the Catskills.

Separation from her parents was the beginning of young Isabella's trials in the *Narrative*. The first of many beatings came from her second owners, who were vexed by her inability to speak English. Her subsequent purchase by a Dutch family meant fewer floggings but created other problems, and she was sold again. Within two years, Isabella was transferred three times.

She grew to womanhood on John I. Dumont's New Paltz farm, where she often did the work of at least two people. She was a field hand, milkmaid, cleaning woman, weaver, cook, and wet nurse. Isabella had the rangy build (she was six feet tall) and hardy vigor of her father. Dumont boasted that his "wench" Bell was "better to me than a *man*—for she will do a good family's washing in the night, and be ready in the morning to go into the field, where she will do as much at raking and binding as my best hands." Yet none of these qualities spared her from the ravages of bondage.

Like all slaves, Isabella longed for freedom, and she knew the appointed date of liberty for New York slaves. Like many slaveholders, John Dumont was loath to lose free labor. When he broke a promise to the "faithful Bell" to free her early for meritorious service, she took matters into her own hands. Carrying her youngest child, who was still an infant, Isabella rose before dawn and walked to freedom. She left her other children tied to servitude by the 1799 and 1817 emancipation laws,[10] and she sought refuge with the Van Wagenen family, who bought out the remainder of her time as a slave and gave her lodging.

In her lifetime, Isabella changed names twice. Not wishing to be known by the name of her previous slaveholders, she adopted the last name Van Wagenen. She again changed her name as the "voices" instructed her in 1843 when she became "an instrument of God" and began her life as a traveling preacher. At that point Isabella Van Wagenen became Sojourner Truth, a woman whose proclaimed mission was to "sojourn" the land and speak God's "truth."

In her speeches, sermons, and lectures Sojourner Truth took parables from everyday life to explain important political and social issues. Her words were peppered with biblical metaphors, symbols, and quotations. In the extemporaneous, spontaneous "stump" speaker tradition popular in antebellum America, few could match Sojourner Truth. Whether trying to persuade farmers in western states on antislavery, communing with her eastern abolitionist friends, detailing her own bondage experience with other blacks, or addressing her favorite audience, the children who often flocked around her, Sojourner captivated her hearers. Her communicative capacity and personal magnetism were subjects of conversation wherever she went. "This unlearned African woman," wrote one Iowa observer, "has a magnetic power over an audience perfectly astounding." Thus, as Sojourner said, "I cannot read a book, but I can read the people."[11]

NORTHERN SLAVERY:
THE AFRICAN-DUTCH PERSPECTIVE

In the early 1600s, New York and New Jersey were part of the Dutch empire of New Netherlands, in which African slavery was the primary labor system. Active and sometimes dominant on the West African coast, Dutch slave traders vied with the Portuguese for control of the Kongo-Angolan ports and introduced bondage in all of their American possessions. Yet the Dutch had no specific policy for establishing slavery, which developed alongside white indentured servitude. When New Netherlands fell to Britain, creating New York and New Jersey in 1664, the "Articles of Capitulation" recognized slavery as a legal institution in the region for the first time.[12]

The English Parliament gave strong support to slavery in these newly acquired colonies, and the institution continued to thrive. Slave owning was so common that the black population of New York was about 14 percent during the colonial era. New York and New Jersey slave codes were similar to those of Southern states and were the harshest in the North. In 1702, the New York Assembly prohibited unauthorized meetings of more than three slaves and gave masters the right to punish slaves at their discretion. In 1705, a strong fugitive slave law was passed. In 1706, New Jersey was the first North American colony to pass a gelding (castration) law for *attempted* rape, although South Carolina soon followed. In New York, reaction to the 1712 New York City Slave Revolt created even harsher restrictions, which extended to both slave and free blacks. Blacks could not own property. Manumission was virtually impossible because the law required payment of 200 pounds for every manumitted slave.[13]

Some historians claim that Dutch slave masters preferred "assimilated" blacks from Curaçao over "proud and treacherous" African-born peoples. In the seventeenth century, Dutch slaves en route to New Netherlands and later New York and New Jersey came by way of Curaçao. But they were not, as some argue, "assimilated." Curaçao, a small island unsuitable for agriculture, was a holding cell, factory, or barracoon for slaves. By 1668 purveyors had even erected a warehouse to store 3,000 Africans and assure their quick delivery to American buyers. Resident domestic slaves were branded to distinguish them from the "saltwater" Africans destined for North and South American markets. These Africans were mainly from Angola, where Holland and Portugal competed for mastery. Portugal's ultimate victory in Africa did not halt Dutch procurement, since the Dutch continued to control Loango while trading on the Gold and Slave coasts. European conflicts and political complications shifted regional origins of African slaves. Nevertheless, Loango-Angola remained a steady supplier throughout the eighteenth century.[14]

African as well as Dutch cultural influences were part of Isabella's background. She was not African born, despite what some scholars have written.[15] But her parents may have been, given Dutch activity in the slave trade, rising imports, and the increase in New York's black population. In the twenty-five years before the War of Independence, Ulster's black population nearly doubled, from 1,100 in 1746 to 2,000 in 1771.[16]

Isabella's first owners, the Hardenberghs, were part of a large family with branches in New York and New Jersey. Their massive landholdings (with five other patentees they claimed 2 million acres) were diminished by squatters, lawsuits, and subdivisions among the family members. Johannes, Jr., was wealthy by eighteenth-century standards, but other Hardenberghs were not. Farming was the general occupation of most Ulster residents.

Timothy Dwight's observation while traveling through the Hudson Valley describes the setting into which Isabella was born:

> The entire region is middling by population, and proportionately there is sufficient agriculture, but the inhabitants seem to be poor. The women commonly walk without shoes, and the numbers of Negroes is large. The latter and the whites speak Dutch generally, so that the traveler imagines himself in the middle of a Dutch colony.

To Moreau de St. Mery, the Dutch were avaricious and indolent. "They almost starve themselves, and treat their slaves miserably," he wrote. The Dutch were also known for their "insular" attitude, reluctance to accept change, and unwillingness to part with their "property." But their typically small holdings meant that they needed only a few slaves. This created a type of slavery that, as Shane White notes, was not *milder* than slavery in the South but "different."[17]

Some early travelers contributed to hoary myths about paternalistic Dutch slavery, believing that slaves were sometimes regarded as "part of the family." Furthermore, the fact that the Dutch had not codified slavery, although they lived under

Anglo-American law, may have allowed for more individual "privileges." In Isabella's home of Ulster County, the rural, quasi-frontier setting necessitated that blacks and whites live in close proximity in ostensible family fashion. But this "functional closeness" did not lead to personal intimacy.[18]

When Holland lost New Netherlands, Dutch settlers retained their land, language, religion (Dutch Reformed), and slaves. In 1776, the Hardenberghs fought for the patriot cause, serving as officers in the Anglo-American conflict. Afterward, they entertained George and Martha Washington as well as De Witt Clinton at their estate, Hardenbergh Hall.[19] Isabella's mother probably served these dignitaries in the house, and her father probably saw to their horses and carriages.

Postwar debates did not weaken slavery in Ulster County as they did in some parts of New York and the North. The Dutch resisted passage of every gradual manumission law. After the War of Independence, European travelers noted that even the poor and the yeomen farmers with only several hundred acres had one or two slaves. Agriculture was diverse. Wheat was a main crop, but tobacco, rye, corn, oats, and flax were also cultivated. Additionally, residents of the Hudson Valley specialized in orchard crops and raised livestock. Sheep, goats, beef cattle, hogs, horses, and dairy cows abounded. Labor was rigorous, and slaves sheared sheep, spun wool, cultivated and harvested crops, treated hay, and performed some skilled labor.

New York slavery was different from bondage in the South because the state lacked long, warm growing seasons, a monocrop, heavily concentrated black populations, and expansive plantations. But large-scale capital investments in lumber, grain, river commerce, and food products created a need for labor, particularly in the colonial era. New York had the largest slave population of any Northern colony. Many slaves labored for a rural elite such as the Ulster Hasbroucks and Hardenberghs. Among families with small investments and few bondspeople, slavery encouraged an indolent, avaricious attitude. Isabella knew both types of bondage, and both extended the longevity of slavery in New York State.[20]

After the war with Britain, emancipation came comparatively quickly in New England and Pennsylvania. When New York formulated its state constitution in 1777, however, manumission had few supporters. Johannes Hardenbergh joined other Ulster delegates in opposing a resolution suggested by Gouverneur Morris that slavery was contrary to natural rights and Christianity. Black participation in the struggle against Britain, Quaker antislavery activity, and formation of the New York Manumission Society in 1785 were the impetus for eventual emancipation. But that year an abolition bill was narrowly defeated, with opposition led by Ulster, Kings, and Richmond counties—all strongly Dutch.[21]

Again despite antislavery advocates' struggle, in 1788 the state legislature passed the first new, comprehensive slave code since 1730. In reaction to proemancipation sentiments, slaveholders began exporting bondspeople out of the state. Undoubtedly some of Isabella's older siblings fell victim to this turn of events, as did her son, Peter, years later. And because of the stipulation that every person enslaved in 1788 was a slave for life, Isabella's parents could entertain no legal hope of freedom in their productive years.[22]

In 1790, 21,000 of New York's 26,000 African-Americans were in bondage. Emancipation debates heated every session of the legislature. In 1797, the year of Isabella's birth, a law that would become effective on July 4, 1799, stipulated that all children born thenceforth would be free but must serve until the age of twenty-eight if male and twenty-five if female. Unfortunately, Isabella was born too early to benefit from this law, which in effect freed no one immediately. Nevertheless, the Hudson River Valley Dutch strongly opposed the measure. These slaveholders, one lawmaker wrote, "raved and swore by *dunder* and *blixen* that we were robbing them of their property. We told them they had none, and could hold none in human flesh."[23]

According to the *Narrative,* having the "best" of masters was no protection against the bitterness of bondage. Isabella was fortunate to spend her first eleven years with her parents and to remain in Ulster County following their separation. Her older siblings were either sold away or given as presents to other Hardenberghs (a common Dutch custom). Her experience illustrates how small landholdings created more community fragmentation and insecurity for slaves than large plantation systems.[24] Her *Narrative* also exemplifies how small-scale slavery meant closer white scrutiny in terms of both labor extracted and personal supervision, which could be arbitrary and absolute.

Isabella's recollection of how slaves lived was typical for rural New York. Most Dutch slaveholders housed slaves in the cellars or attics of their homes. Males and females often slept in common in these barracklike quarters. She recalls in the *Narrative* the dampness of the cheerless, dark Hardenbergh cellar that she, Elizabeth, James, and brother Peter called home. Such functional closeness between master and slave left bondspeople with little privacy.

Perhaps the most ruthless contradiction in interpreting Dutch slavery as mild or paternalistic relates to emancipation. Before 1785, slaveholders freeing slaves posted 200 pounds security against slave dependency on the community. After this law was changed, some masters freed slaves past their prime but not yet fifty as a means of avoiding their care during illness or old age.[25] Such a fate awaited Isabella's parents. The forests of Ulster County housed many elderly, infirm former slaves dependent on goodwill in inclement weather and the sun's warmth in fair seasons. Rather than care for "worn out" slaves, Dutch slave masters, like Southern planters, put them out "to pasture," like so many cattle.

Daniel D. Tompkins, New York Manumission Society member and New York State governor until he assumed the vice presidency under James Monroe, referred to his most important act, the total abolition of slavery, in 1817. He had called for the "gradual and ultimate extinction of . . . slavery, that reproach of a free people," in his 1811 annual message. After fits and starts, the legislature surpassed his expectations. A bill was passed providing that all blacks born before July 4, 1799, were free as of July 4, 1827—ten years hence.[26] This law would have freed Isabella from bondage, but before her freedom legally took effect, she boldly liberated herself.

MEANINGS OF FREEDOM, BONDS OF AFFECTION, AND SPIRITUAL AWAKENINGS

A sense of community and the persistence of a dynamic, adaptive cultural ethos are vital considerations in interpreting the effects of bondage on African-American slaves. Two primary institutional components of community and culture are the family and a belief system. The family represents collective accountability, loyalty, bonds of affection, and, in the ideal, stability and continuity. A belief system brings order to human actions, provides understanding of the cosmic world, and casts what Clifford Geertz calls a "lunar light" over the temporal world.[27] Although based on faith, a belief system can be manipulated and internalized to mitigate against the raw power of an authoritarian, secular force. Isabella's life and those of other African-Dutch slaves can be viewed from this perspective.

Some scholars represent the New York slave family as facing difficulties so insurmountable that it had no significance as a cohesive force. In rural New York, population imbalance, forced separation, forced matings, frequent sales, and loss of control over children's instruction were among the factors that made bondage "little short of devastating in its impact on the black family."[28] Sojourner Truth's *Narrative* seemingly supports this grim assessment. Her mother's children were taken away, and in 1826 Isabella left her own children at the Dumonts' to pursue her liberty. In 1829 she departed Ulster County with her son Peter for New York City, seeking a better life.

However, that is only the shell of the story. Interpreting the black family primarily through the debilitating features of bondage and concluding that slavery destroyed the family unit says more about the limitations of such historical writing than about the slave family. Such a viewpoint avoids important questions about black people's challenge to white hegemony and, in particular, how they acted on their common beliefs about institutional arrangements. And it makes it seem that since masters did not *treat* slaves as if they formed family units, the slave family was not a reality. Even Olive Gilbert, to whom Isabella dictated the *Narrative,* reflects this view—in her words, the slave family appears weak and pathetic.

But Isabella's experience offers a long-range assessment of the meaning of family and an African-American interpretation of the historical value of family connections. Her experience is a Northern example of how families struggled and bonded under oppressive conditions, something already demonstrated in studies of the slave family in the South. Isabella's mother, "Mau-mau Bett," was the preserver of family bonds. She kept alive her children's memory by teaching Isabella and her brother their siblings' names and recounting both "endearing" and "harrowing" circumstances of her brief time with them. Isabella's relationship with her father, James, was both fortuitous and tragic. Following her sale, Isabella was close enough for James to maintain contact with her as long as his health allowed. Insofar as he could, James offered a father's protection by securing a more tolerant owner than the Englishman who beat his daughter.

After her mother's death, Isabella sadly witnessed James's decline. Her account of him during his last days—lame, blind, alone, and homeless—and her helplessness to relieve his agony, constitutes the most moving passage in an unusually poignant narrative.

Isabella's relationship with her own children further mirrors family relations among African-Dutch bondspeople. Gradual emancipation bound her children to the Dumonts—and she could not have provided a home for them anyway, since as a domestic in Ulster County and in New York City Isabella resided with her employers. Yet she was an attentive mother, frequently visiting the children and later fulfilling her promise to provide a home for her whole family.[29]

Like those of Mau-mau Bett, Sojourner Truth's family connections are testaments to the resiliency of the slave family. But the *Narrative* also suggests how African-Americans found ways of circumventing disruptive forces. For example, Elizabeth's impressing upon Isabella the names and characteristics of her lost siblings enabled Isabella to recognize and reunite with some of them later. Also, nomenclature was an important means of recalling kinship and ancestry as well as encouraging community ties. Four of Isabella's known children who survived childhood—Diana, Elizabeth, Peter, and Sophia—were named for her parents and siblings, thus creating a collective identity and re-creating her family. Of two other children mentioned but not yet traced, one was named James, for her father. As mentioned earlier, for Sojourner, naming was truly a symbolic act fraught with timeless meaning. She named herself twice, and each change was a special self-interpretation in her creating of her own identity.

Familial influence in the *Narrative* is further exemplified through parental instruction and guidance. Knowing what fate awaited the young Isabella and her brother, Elizabeth prepared them spiritually by imparting beliefs that encouraged optimism and a reason for being. The out-of-doors was their temple. "Under the sparkling vault of heaven," Elizabeth taught her children "there is a God, who hears and sees you, . . . He lives in the sky." She taught them to call upon God for help "when you are beaten, or cruelly treated, or fall into any trouble." She also cautioned them about good behavior, so God would heed their appeals. Although Isabella strayed from this advice as a youth, it penetrated her consciousness. As an adult and mother, she returned to the ancient, mystical faith of Mau-mau Bett, drawing courage from her assurance that a power beyond that of slaveholders existed.

Isabella's spiritual realm emerged both from her mother's teachings and from the shadow of Whitsuntide, the Dutch Pentecost celebration described in the *Narrative* as "Pingster" (Pinkster). This annual "Feast of the Holy Trinity," popular in Europe, was brought to New Netherlands. New York slaves grafted onto Pinkster meanings more suitable to their own needs and merged it with their African heritage. Young bondspeople, like Isabella, considered its secular aspect paramount because Pinkster was a week of frolic and abandon. Booths were set up where fish, cakes, fruit, meat, cider, and beer were sold. Slaves dressed up in finery. A "king" usually led a parade. Slaves sang, danced, drummed, fiddled, gambled, smoked, and drank heavily.[30]

Among the slaves' Pinkster rituals, music, masquerades, spectacle, and intensely symbolic dances were reminiscent of African festivals. The king leading the procession, accompanied by his followers and receiving tribute from black (and sometimes white) subjects, exemplifies a hierarchical system strongly adhered to in the Kongo-Angola and Gold Coast regions of Africa. It is no unrealistic leap to suggest that African-Dutch slaves from these regions syncretized elements of their ancient society with a Dutch holiday.[31]

It was likewise no accident that Isabella's religious transformation in the *Narrative* coincided with Pinkster. This celebration of the Holy Ghost permitted black exhortation and autonomous religious worship without baptism or church membership. Isabella symbolically describes her vision and spiritual awakening as "God's breath." Similarly, Pentecost traditions included the evocation of a "Holy Wind" that would rush through the heart, provoking tongues of fire, speaking in tongues, and spiritual telepathy. Isabella's conversion was grounded in traditions of Africanity and Christianity alike.

Much has been written about African-American slave narratives and the narrators' sense of empowerment through literacy—the desire to "talk to books." According to Henry Louis Gates, Jr., for example, African-born James Albert Gronniosaw used literacy to negate his feelings of inferiority because of his blackness. Acquisition of literacy for Frederick Douglass was a door to freedom and personal recognition. For many eighteenth- and nineteenth-century black writers, this most important of Western technologies "humanized" them in the eyes of white bourgeois society. Gates maintains that

> the recording of an authentic black voice, a voice of deliverance from the deafening discursive silence which an "enlightened" Europe cited as proof of the absence of the African's humanity was the millennial instrument of transformation through which the African would become the European, the slave become the ex-slave, the brute animal become the human being.[32]

Possessing literacy placed Africans and black Americans within the cultural purview of Western society in a direct correlation with the Enlightenment's political and educational philosophy about the "rights of man." The connection between literacy and freedom was not lost on slaveholders, which is why most Southern states forbade reading and writing among bondspeople. Even the "friends" of the slaves, the abolitionists, articulated this perspective.[33] Notions of what constituted a "civilized" person were subsequently imbibed by many former slaves who mastered the written word. Slaves who purchased freedom, fugitives, and free blacks often sought to prove their humanity to white America through this process.

But not all narratives were authored by literate blacks. It is important to remember that for African-Americans who professed a spiritual calling, extraliterary forms were a more meaningful aesthetic vehicle and a source of power outside the prejudices of the patriarchal order. Furthermore, nonliterary visual and oral expression tied spiritual narratives closer to traditional African aesthetic practices and represented more authentically the collective antebellum black experience and voice—that of a people socially and politically marginalized, almost completely excluded from both formal and informal educational structure.

Although she could not read, Sojourner Truth memorized most of the Bible and quoted it at length throughout her life. Combined with her intuitive religious insights, this kind of orality reflected her African heritage more than her American environment. Her mother's mysticism did not come from an institutional church. Taking her children out at night to commune with the stars, moon, and a god was not taught Elizabeth by the Dutch Reformed Church. These customs were undoubtedly vestiges of African ontology.

Memory and orality represent the African practices through which the past was conventionally preserved. Such methods of communicating knowledge and history are closely tied to visionary literacy, which in the case of the spiritual narrative, does not require the technical skills of reading and writing. In essence, the lack of secular literacy forces the spiritual narrator to rely completely on another discourse. This reliance in turn sharpens and refines the visual experience in its spiritual context. Books did not speak to Sojourner Truth. As she said on more than one occasion, "You read books, I talk to God."

Isabella's graphic portrayal of her conversion, her intimate contact with a divine being, and the intensity of her soliloquies with this supernatural presence are as deeply reminiscent of African spiritual belief systems as of Pentecost. Elements of spirit possession and the importance of spiritual transcendence characterize Isabella's experience and sense of mission.

African religion emphasizes visual spirit embodiment and visionary trances via spirit possession as living examples of the sacred world. Spirit-embodying objects have recently been found on graves in black cemeteries in heavily Dutch Bergen County, New Jersey; Staten Island, New York; and New York City. Broken pieces of white pottery found on graves in the South and pipes coming out of graves in the North belonged to funerary rites symbolizing the *flight* of the spirit from the body. The shells, glass, and other objects reflecting light found on these graves materially express the *flash* of the spirit separating from the human form and traveling to the sacred world (underwater), where all is light and brilliance.[34]

In West African spirituality, the state of ecstatic vision contains a commonality: "temporary alienation of the very being of the person concerned." Achieving the mystical vision and communicating with the spirit means "leaving in order to return," and also "letting go of oneself totally in order to recover oneself anew." It is death and resurrection. Among some African peoples, the "call" of the spirit occurs spontaneously and usually at celebrations or ceremonies. This spiritual calling creates a second, sacred consciousness which coexists with personal loyalties and responsibilities.[35]

Isabella was armed with the "Holy Wind" of Whitsuntide, spirit communication, and a "call" revealed through visual perceptions. Together they were the key to her religious and political transformation which in the *Narrative* cannot be separated. Both empowered her to challenge secular authority.

When Isabella confronted those responsible for her son's illegal sale to an Alabama family and demanded his return, she had no money, no education, no transportation, not even a pair of shoes. But she felt the surge of power through justice for which she became famous. In the years before she began to travel and preach, her liberty, conversion experience, and her sense of moral superiority gave her a strength beyond her social and economic power. Speaking of her determination to regain her son Peter, she exclaimed, "Oh my God! I know'd I'd have him again. Why, I felt so *tall within*—I felt as if the *power of a nation* was with me."

What a prophetic statement for Sojourner Truth to make in 1850! She was not yet a famous lecturer but was merely attempting to tell her story to support herself and to assist the abolitionist cause. Yet the majesty, vitality, and endurance she summoned in standing up for her rights as a free woman were later reflected in her work as a social reformer, counselor of freedpeople, and sponsor of a black movement to the west. Through her will, her faith, and her love, she indeed possessed "the power of a nation."

"INDELICATE" SUBJECTS—
BLACK WOMANHOOD AND SEXUALITY

Gender-specific devaluation is an implicit, underlying theme in Isabella's story. It is peculiar that Olive Gilbert's censoring of Isabella's story is strongest in the female "sphere" and in sexuality. Gilbert decided, or perhaps was told, to omit certain details about Isabella's life. The *Narrative* is silent on many of Isabella's "long series of trials," says Gilbert, "not for want of facts" but "from motives of delicacy."

Relationships between black and white women during slavery were often volatile. Issues of power, complicated by sexual undertones, led to white female hostility. Only occasionally did the two races coexist peacefully, and hardly ever amicably. Like all black women, Isabella was exploited as a laborer, and her sex exacerbated her oppression in ways significantly different from what men experienced. Female slaves' economic productivity was measured in terms of reproduction as much as labor output. Their womanness was considered an open sexual invitation to white men, and if white women objected, fault was placed with black women.

Feminist historians such as Barbara Welter maintain that a cult of true womanhood existed in the nineteenth century. This ideal of white womanhood had "four cardinal virtues—piety, purity, submissiveness and domesticity." Literary scholar Hazel Carby has analyzed this ideal as a societal formula that contrasted white women with black women. What she argues for the South is also true of the North.

The guiding pillars of the concept of true womanhood were piety and purity—qualities to which neither Isabella nor other black women could ever aspire because black women were objectified as sexual beings and laborers. Sensuality, sexuality, passion, lust—whatever one calls it—was a condition that patriarchal white men considered base and immoral in *their* women for obvious reasons. Such "vulgar" sentiments were fit only for inferior females, namely black women. As Carby points out, this dichotomy kept white males in control of two female spheres. Slaves inherited the status of their mothers and "gave birth to property." White women reproduced the children who strengthened patriarchal order and inherited its power.[36]

The sexual license of white men and separation from their children were distinct color-coded realities for black womanhood in nineteenth-century America.[37] And the complicity of white women in this process clouds the common experience of gender. For many white women, slaveholders or not, perceptions of white female piety and purity versus black women's immorality and promiscuity legitimized a double standard. In their minds, Isabella could not possess "true womanhood." And, if not a "true woman," she could feel no emotional pangs on being separated from her children. If not a "true woman," she could be ignored, even laughed at. From this perspective, Isabella was not mother, daughter, sister, wife, or woman.

Yet Isabella forces us to look beyond "victimology" in rejection of white constructions of what is a mother and a "true" woman. Indeed she proves to be both, and she commands attention. Her love of family, her sense of virtue, and her claim to pietistic superiority were the weapons she employed to resist the stereotype of what it meant to be poor, black, slave, and female.

The efforts of antislavery writers and activists to "uplift" black women and present them favorably as "moral" beings to a doubting public may in some measure have interfered with the African-American woman's attempt to tell her story frankly and confront issues of sexuality openly. Former slave Harriet Jacobs had the advantage over Sojourner Truth in this sense at least, because she was literate. Jean Fagan Yellin correctly states that Sojourner did not deal with sexuality in her *Narrative*.[38] Had she, like Jacobs, been able to write, Sojourner could have told her story more fully. But given her lack of education and the conventional views of her amanuensis, this was not possible. Nevertheless, anyone who studies the *Narrative* and is familiar with the plight of female slaves can easily read between the lines—and should do so whenever reading narratives of black women unable to write for themselves.

While Olive Gilbert's concepts of "true womanhood" affected how she discussed "delicate" subjects in the *Narrative,* Sojourner Truth was not modest about the sexual politics of slavery. She scoffed at white ideals of womanhood and challenged the patriarchal nature of American society. Sexuality was for her an open issue because she, like many slave women, separated the physical body from the spiritual self. This separation represented a means of resisting the effects of sexual exploitation.

In 1858, Sojourner Truth faced proslavery hecklers and unabashedly proved that she was indeed a woman. Men in the audience expressed doubt about her sex and demanded that "Sojourner submit her breast to the inspection of some of the ladies present." The women were "ashamed and indignant at such a proposition." But "Sojourner exposed her naked breasts" and said that she said had "suckled many a white babe, to the exclusion of her own." The shame, said Sojourner, was not hers but theirs. As Harryette Mullen points out, Sojourner's defiance was empowering for both her and her embarrassed white sisters. She not only denied "social propriety its oppressive power to define, limit, or regulate" but also scoffed at "the conventions of femininity."[39] Above all, she assumed a heroic, superior posture over both the white women and the men.

Sex was considered "indelicate" by women as well as men. Even Lydia Maria Child, in prefacing Harriet Jacobs's work, was moved to apologize for its specifically sexual nature. Child recognized that she faced accusations of "indecorum" because Jacobs's narrative dealt with "delicate," or what others called "indelicate," subjects. Sexuality as a theme was usually "veiled." But Child believed it was time to acquaint the public with the more "monstrous features of bondage." "I do this," she wrote, "for the sake of my sisters in bondage, who are suffering wrongs so foul, that our ears are too delicate to listen to them."[40]

In the final analysis, the *Narrative of Sojourner Truth* must be evaluated more for what it says than for what it leaves unsaid. Sojourner substantiated its contents many times over in speeches and recollections. Isabella emerged as Sojourner Truth largely because of the test of her early life, her endurance, and her talents. By dictating her slave *Narrative,* working for the abolition of bondage, being an outspoken friend and critic of women's rights, and fighting a lonely crusade for African-American self-determination, Sojourner Truth wrote herself into history.

Narrative of Sojourner Truth

❀

Sweet is the virgin honey, though the wild bee store it in a reed;
And bright the jewelled band that circleth an Ethiop's arm;
Pure are the grains of gold in the turbid stream of the Ganges;
And fair the living flowers that spring from the dull cold sod.
Wherefore, thou gentle student, bend thine ear to my speech,
For I also am as thou art; our hearts can commune together;
To meanest matters will I stoop, for mean is the lot of mortal;
I will rise to noblest themes, for the soul hath a heritage of glory.

Narrative of

SOJOURNER TRUTH

HER BIRTH AND PARENTAGE

❂

THE SUBJECT of this biography, SOJOURNER TRUTH, as she now calls herself—but whose name, originally, was Isabella—was born, as near as she can now calculate, between the years 1797 and 1800.[1] She was the daughter of James and Betsey, slaves of one Colonel Ardinburgh, Hurley, Ulster County, New York.[2]

Colonel Ardinburgh belonged to that class of people called Low Dutch.

Of her first master, she can give no account, as she must have been a mere infant when he died; and she, with her parents and some ten or twelve other fellow human chattels, became the legal property of his son, Charles Ardinburgh. She distinctly remembers hearing her father and mother say, that their lot was a fortunate one, as Master Charles was the best of the family,—being, comparatively speaking, a kind master to his slaves.

James and Betsey having, by their faithfulness, docility, and respectful behavior, won his particular regard, received from him particular favors—among which was a lot of land, lying back on the slope of a mountain, where, by improving the pleasant evenings and Sundays, they managed to raise a little tobacco, corn, or flax; which they exchanged for extras, in the articles of food or clothing for themselves and children. She has no remembrance that Saturday afternoon was ever added to their own time, as it is by *some* masters in the Southern States.

ACCOMMODATIONS

Among Isabella's earliest recollections was the removal of her master, Charles Ardinburgh, into his new house, which he had built for a hotel, soon after the decease of his father. A cellar, under this hotel, was assigned to his slaves, as their sleeping apartment,—all the slaves he possessed, of both sexes, sleeping (as is quite common in a state of slavery) in the same room. She carries in her mind, to this day, a vivid picture of this dismal chamber; its only lights consisting of a few panes of glass, through which she thinks the sun never shone, but with thrice reflected rays; and the space between the loose boards of the floor, and the uneven earth below, was often filled with mud and water, the uncomfortable splashings of which were as annoying as its noxious vapors must have been chilling and fatal to health. She shudders, even now, as she goes back in memory, and revisits this cellar, and sees its inmates, of both sexes and all ages, sleeping on those damp boards, like the horse, with a little straw and a blanket; and she wonders not at the rheumatisms, and fever-sores, and palsies, that distorted the limbs and racked the bodies of those fellow-slaves in after-life. Still, she does not attribute this cruelty—for cruelty it certainly is, to be so unmindful of the health and comfort of any being, leaving entirely out of sight his more important part, his everlasting interests,—so much to any innate or constitutional cruelty of the master, as to that gigantic inconsistency, that inherited habit among slaveholders, of expecting a willing and intelligent obedience from the slave, because he is a MAN—at the same time every thing belonging to the soul-harrowing system does its best to crush the last vestige of a man within him; and when it *is* crushed, and often before, he is denied the comforts of life, on the plea that he knows neither the want nor the use of them, and because he is considered to be little more or little *less* than a beast.

HER BROTHERS AND SISTERS

Isabella's father was very tall and straight, when young, which gave him the name of "Bomefree"—low Dutch for tree—at least, this is Sojourner's pronunciation of it—and by this name he usually went. The most familiar appellation of her mother was "Mau-mau Bett." She was the mother of some ten or twelve children; though Sojourner is far from knowing the exact number of her brothers and sisters; she being the youngest, save one, and all older than herself having been sold before her remembrance. She was privileged to behold six of them while she remained a slave.

Of the two that immediately preceded her in age, a boy of five years, and a girl of three, who were sold when she was an infant, she heard much; and she wishes that all who would fain believe that slave parents have not natural affection for their offspring could have listened as *she* did, while Bomefree and Mau-mau Bett,—their dark cellar lighted by a blazing pine-knot,—would sit for hours, recalling and recounting every endearing, as well as harrowing circumstance that taxed memory could supply, from the histories of those dear departed ones, of whom they had been robbed, and for whom their hearts still bled. Among the rest, they would relate how the little boy, on the last morning he was with them, arose with the birds, kindled a fire, calling for his Mau-mau to "come, for all was now ready for her"—little dreaming of the dreadful separation which was so near at hand, but of which his parents had an uncertain, but all the more cruel foreboding. There was snow on the ground, at the time of which we are speaking; and a large old-fashioned sleigh was seen to drive up to the door of the late Col. Ardinburgh. This event was noticed with childish pleasure by the unsuspicious boy; but when he was taken and put into the sleigh, and saw his little sister actually shut and locked into the sleigh-box, his eyes were at once opened to their intentions; and, like a frightened deer, he sprang from the sleigh, and running into the house, concealed himself under a bed. But this availed him little. He was reconveyed to the sleigh, and separated for ever from those whom God had constituted his natural guardians and protectors, and who should have found him, in return, a stay and a staff to them in their declining years. But I make no comments on facts like these, knowing that the heart of every slave parent will make its own comments, involuntarily and correctly, as soon as each heart shall make the case its own. Those who are not parents will draw their conclusions from the promptings of humanity and philanthropy:—these, enlightened by reason and revelation, are also unerring.

HER RELIGIOUS INSTRUCTION

Isabella and Peter, her youngest brother, remained, with their parents, the legal property of Charles Ardinburgh till his decease, which took place when Isabella was near nine years old.[3]

After this event, she was often surprised to find her mother in tears; and when, in her simplicity, she inquired, "Mau-mau, what makes you cry?" she would answer, "Oh, my child, I am thinking of your brothers and sisters that have been sold away from me." And she would proceed to detail many circumstances respecting them. But Isabella long since concluded that it was the impending fate of her only remaining children, which her mother but too well understood, even then, that called up those memories from the past, and made them crucify her heart afresh.

In the evening, when her mother's work was done, she would sit down under the sparkling vault of heaven, and calling her children to her, would talk to them of the only Being that could effectually aid or protect them. Her teachings were delivered in Low Dutch, her only language, and, translated into English, ran nearly as follows:—

"My children, there is a God, who hears and sees you." "A *God*, mau-mau! Where does he live?" asked the children. "He lives in the sky," she replied; "and when you are beaten, or cruelly treated, or fall into any trouble, you must ask help of him, and he will always hear and help you." She taught them to kneel and say the Lord's prayer. She entreated them to refrain from lying and stealing, and to strive to obey their masters.

At times, a groan would escape her, and she would break out in the language of the Psalmist—"Oh Lord, how long?" "Oh Lord, how long?" And in reply to Isabella's question—"What ails you, mau-mau?" her only answer was, "Oh, a good deal ails me"—"Enough ails me." Then again, she would point them to the stars, and say, in her peculiar language, "Those are the same stars, and that is the same moon, that look down upon your brothers and sisters, and which they see as they look up to them, though they are ever so far away from us, and each other."

Thus, in her humble way, did she endeavor to show them their Heavenly Father, as the only being who could protect them in their perilous condition; at the same time, she would strengthen and brighten the chain of family affection, which she trusted extended itself sufficiently to connect the widely scattered members of her precious flock. These instructions of the mother were treasured up and held sacred by Isabella, as our future narrative will show.

THE AUCTION

At length, the never-to-be-forgotten day of the terrible auction arrived, when the "slaves, horses, and other cattle" of Charles Ardinburgh, deceased, were to be put under the hammer, and again change masters. Not only Isabella and Peter, but their mother, was now destined to the auction block, and would have been struck off with the rest to the highest bidder, but for the following circumstance: A question arose among the heirs, "Who shall be burthened with Bomefree, when we have sent away his faithful Mau-mau Bett?" He was becoming weak and infirm; his limbs were painfully rheumatic and distorted—more from exposure and hardship than from old age, though he was several years older than Mau-mau Bett; he was no longer considered of value, but must soon be a burthen and care to some one. After some contention on the point at issue, none being willing to be burthened with him, it was finally agreed, as most expedient for the heirs, that the price of Mau-mau Bett should be sacrificed, and she receive her freedom, on condition that she take care of and support her faithful James,—faithful, not only to her as a husband, but proverbially faithful as a slave to those who would not willingly sacrifice a dollar for *his* comfort, now that he had commenced his descent into the dark vale of decrepitude and suffering. This important decision was received as joyful news indeed to our ancient couple, who were the objects of it, and who were trying to prepare their hearts for a severe struggle, and one altogether new to them, as they had never before been separated; for, though ignorant, helpless, crushed in spirit, and weighed down with hardship and cruel bereavement, they were still human, and their human hearts beat within them with as true an affection as ever caused a human heart to beat. And their anticipated separation now, in the decline of life, after the last

child had been torn from them, must have been truly appalling.
Another privilege was granted them—that of remaining occu-
pants of the same dark, humid cellar I have before described:
otherwise, they were to support themselves as they best could.
And as her mother was still able to do considerable work, and
her father a little, they got on for some time very comfortably.
The strangers who rented the house were humane people, and
very kind to them; they were not rich, and owned no slaves.
How long this state of things continued, we are unable to say,
as Isabella had not then sufficiently cultivated her organ of time
to calculate years, or even weeks or hours. But she thinks her
mother must have lived several years after the death of Master
Charles. She remembers going to visit her parents some three or
four times before the death of her mother, and a good deal of
time seemed to her to intervene between each visit.[4]

At length, her mother's health began to decline—a fever-sore
made its ravages on one of her limbs, and the palsy began to
shake her frame; still, she and James tottered about, picking up
a little here and there, which, added to the mites contributed by
their kind neighbors, sufficed to sustain life, and drive famine
from the door.

DEATH OF MAU-MAU BETT

One morning, in early autumn, (from the reason above-
mentioned, we cannot tell what year,) Mau-mau Bett told James
she would make him a loaf of rye-bread, and get Mrs. Simmons,
their kind neighbor, to bake it for them, as she would bake that
forenoon. James told her he had engaged to rake after the cart
for his neighbors that morning; but before he commenced, he
would pole off some apples from a tree near, which they were
allowed to gather; and if she could get some of them baked with

the bread, it would give it a nice relish for their dinner. He beat off the apples and soon after, saw Mau-mau Bett come out and gather them up.

At the blowing of the horn for dinner, he groped his way into his cellar, anticipating his humble, but warm and nourishing meal; when, lo! instead of being cheered by the sight and odor of fresh-baked bread and the savory apples, his cellar seemed more cheerless than usual, and at first neither sight nor sound met eye or ear. But, on groping his way through the room, his staff, which he used as a pioneer to go before, and warn him of danger, seemed to be impeded in its progress, and a low, gurgling, choking sound proceeded from the object before him, giving him the first intimation of the truth as it was, that Mau-mau Bett, his bosom companion, the only remaining member of his large family, had fallen in a fit of the palsy, and lay helpless and senseless on the earth! Who among us, located in pleasant homes, surrounded with every comfort, and so many kind and sympathizing friends, can picture to ourselves the dark and desolate state of poor old James—penniless, weak, lame, and nearly blind, as he was at the moment he found his companion was removed from him, and he was left alone in the world, with no one to aid, comfort, or console him? for she never revived again, and lived only a few hours after being discovered senseless by her poor bereaved James.

LAST DAYS OF BOMEFREE

Isabella and Peter were permitted to see the remains of their mother laid in their last narrow dwelling, and to make their bereaved father a little visit, ere they returned to their servitude. And most piteous were the lamentations of the poor old man, when, at last, *they* also were obliged to bid him "Farewell!" Juan

Fernandes, on his desolate island, was not so pitiable an object as this poor lame man. Blind and crippled, he was too super-annuated to think for a moment of taking care of himself, and he greatly feared no persons would interest themselves in his behalf. "Oh," he would exclaim, "I had thought God would take me first,—Mau-mau was so much smarter than I, and could get about and take care of herself;—and I am *so old,* and *so helpless.* What *is* to become of me? I can't do any thing more—my children are all gone, and here I am left helpless and alone." "And then, as I was taking leave of him," said his daughter, in relating it, "he raised his voice, and cried aloud like a child—*Oh, how he* DID *cry!* I HEAR it *now*—and remember it as well as if it were but yesterday—*poor old man! ! !* He thought *God* had done it all—and my heart bled within me at the sight of his misery. He begged me to get permission to come and see him some-times, which I readily and heartily promised him." But when all had left him, the Ardinburghs, having some feeling left for their faithful and favorite slave, "took turns about" in keeping him—permitting him to stay a few weeks at one house, ͟ᴅ then awhile at another, and so around. If, when he made a removal, the place where he was going was not too far off, he took up his line of march, staff in hand, and asked for no assistance. If it was twelve or twenty miles, they gave him a ride. While he was living in this way, Isabella was twice permitted to visit him. Another time she walked twelve miles, and carried her infant in her arms to see him, but when she reached the place where she hoped to find him, he had just left for a place some twenty miles distant, and she never saw him more. The last time she *did* see him, she found him seated on a rock, by the road-side, alone, and far from any house. He was then migrating from the house of one Ardinburgh to that of another, several miles distant. His hair was white like wool—he was almost blind—and his gait was more a creep than a walk—but the weather was warm and pleasant, and he did not dislike the journey. When Isabella

addressed him, he recognized her voice, and was exceeding glad
to see her. He was assisted to mount the wagon, was carried back
to the famous cellar of which we have spoken, and there they
held their last earthly conversation. He again, as usual, bewailed
his loneliness,—spoke in tones of anguish of his many children,
saying, "They are all taken away from me! I have now not one
to give me a cup of cold water—why should I live and not die?"
Isabella, whose heart yearned over her father, and who would
have made any sacrifice to have been able to be with, and take
care of him, tried to comfort, by telling him that "she had heard
the white folks say, that all the slaves in the State would be freed
in ten years, and that then she would come and take care of
him." "I would take just as good care of you as Mau-mau
would, if she was here"—continued Isabel. "Oh, my child,"
replied he, "I cannot *live* that long." "Oh *do,* daddy, do live, and
I will take such *good* care of you," was her rejoinder. She now
says, "Why, I thought then, in my ignorance, that he *could* live,
if he *would*. I just as much thought so, as I ever thought *any* thing
in my life—and I *insisted* on his living: but he shook his head, and
insisted he could not."

But, before Bomefree's good constitution would yield either
to age, exposure, or a strong desire to die, the Ardinburghs again
tired of him, and offered freedom to two old slaves—Cæsar,
brother of Mau-mau Bett, and his wife Betsey—on condition
that they should take care of James. (I was about to say, "their
brother-in-law"—but as slaves are neither *husbands* nor *wives* in
law, the idea of their being brothers-in-law is truly ludicrous.)
And although they were too old and infirm to take care of
themselves, (Cæsar having been afflicted for a long time with
fever-sores, and his wife with the jaundice,) they eagerly accepted the boon of freedom, which had been the life-long desire
of their souls—though at a time when emancipation was to them
little more than destitution, and was a freedom more to be
desired by the master than the slave. Sojourner declares of the

slaves in their ignorance, that "their thoughts are no longer than her finger."

DEATH OF BOMEFREE

A rude cabin, in a lone wood, far from any neighbors, was granted to our freed friends, as the only assistance they were now to expect. Bomefree, from this time, found his poor needs hardly supplied, as his new providers were scarce able to administer to their *own* wants. However, the time drew near when things were to be decidedly worse rather than better; for they had not been together long, before Betty died, and shortly after, Cæsar followed her to "that bourne from whence no traveller returns"—leaving poor James again desolate, and more helpless than ever before; as, this time, there was no kind family in the house, and the Ardinburghs no longer invited him to their homes. Yet, lone, blind, and helpless as he was, James for a time lived on. One day, an aged colored woman, named Soan, called at his shanty, and James besought her, in the most moving manner, even with tears, to tarry awhile and wash and mend him up, so that he might once more be decent and comfortable; for he was suffering dreadfully with the filth and vermin that had collected upon him.

Soan was herself an emancipated slave, old and weak, with no one to care for her; and she lacked the courage to undertake a job of such seeming magnitude, fearing she might herself get sick, and perish there without assistance; and with great reluctance, and a heart swelling with pity, as she afterwards declared, she felt obliged to leave him in his wretchedness and filth. And shortly after her visit, this faithful slave, this deserted wreck of humanity, was found on his miserable pallet, frozen and stiff in death. The kind angel had come at last, and relieved him of the many miseries that his fellow-man had heaped upon him. Yes, he had died, chilled and starved, with none to speak a kindly word, or do a kindly deed for him, in that last dread hour of need!

The news of his death reached the ears of John Ardinburgh, a grandson of the old Colonel; and he declared that "Bomefree, who had ever been a kind and faithful slave, should now have a *good* funeral." And now, gentle reader, what think you constituted a good funeral? Answer—some black paint for the coffin, and—a jug of ardent spirits! What a compensation for a life of toil, of patient submission to repeated robberies of the most aggravated kind, and, also, far more than murderous neglect! ! Mankind often vainly attempt to atone for unkindness or cruelty to the living, by honoring the same after death;—but John Ardinburgh undoubtedly meant *his* pot of paint and jug of whiskey should act as an opiate on his slaves, rather than on his own seared conscience.

COMMENCEMENT OF ISABELLA'S TRIALS IN LIFE

Having seen the sad end of her parents, so far as it relates to *this* earthly life, we will return with Isabella to that memorable auction which threatened to separate her father and mother. A slave auction is a terrible affair to its victims, and its incidents and consequences are graven on their hearts as with a pen of burning steel.

At this memorable time, Isabella was struck off, for the sum of one hundred dollars, to one John Nealy, of Ulster County, New York;[5] and she has an impression that in this sale she was connected with a lot of sheep. She was now nine years of age, and her trials in life may be dated from this period. She says, with emphasis, *"Now the war begun."* She could only talk Dutch—and the Nealy's could only talk English. Mr. Nealy could *understand* Dutch, but Isabel and her mistress could neither of them understand the language of the other—and this, of itself, was a formidable obstacle in the way of a *good* understanding between them, and for some time was a fruitful source of dissatisfaction to the mistress, and of punishment and suffering to Isabella. She says, "If they sent me for a frying-pan, not knowing what they meant, perhaps I carried them the pot-hooks and trammels. Then, oh! how angry mistress would be with me!" Then she suffered *"terribly—terribly,"* with the cold. During the winter her feet were badly frozen, for want of proper covering. They gave her plenty to eat, and also a plenty of whippings. One Sunday morning, in particular, she was told to go to the barn; on going there, she found her master with a bundle of rods, prepared in the embers, and bound together with cords. When he had tied her hands together before her, he gave her the most cruel whipping she was ever tortured with. He whipped her till the flesh was deeply lacerated, and the blood streamed from her wounds—and the scars remain to the present day, to testify to the fact. "And now," she says, "when I hear 'em tell of whipping women on the bare flesh, it makes *my* flesh crawl, and my very hair rise on my head! Oh! my God!" she continues, "what a way is this of treating human beings?" In these hours of her extremity, she did not forget the instructions of her mother, to go to God in all her trials, and every affliction; and she not only remembered, but obeyed; going to Him, "and telling him all—and asking him if he thought it was right," and begging him to protect and shield her from her persecutors.

She always asked with an unwavering faith that she should receive just what she plead for,—"And now," she says, "though it seems *curious,* I do not remember ever asking for any thing but what I got it. And I always received it as an answer to my prayers. When I got beaten, I never knew it long enough beforehand to pray; and I always thought if I only had *had* time to pray God

for help, I should have escaped the beating." She had no idea
God had any knowledge of her thoughts, save what she told
him; or heard her prayers, unless they were spoken audibly. And
consequently, she could not pray unless she had time and opportunity to go by herself, where she could talk to God without
being overheard.

TRIALS CONTINUED

When she had been at Mr. Nealy's several months, she began to
beg God most earnestly to send her father to her, and as soon as
she commenced to pray, she began as confidently to look for his
coming, and ere it was long, to her great joy, he came. She had
no opportunity to speak to him of the troubles that weighed so
heavily on her spirit, while he remained; but when he left, she
followed him to the gate, and unburdened her heart to him,
inquiring if he could not do something to get her a new and
better place? In this way the slaves often assist each other, by
ascertaining who are kind to their slaves, comparatively; and
then using their influence to get such an one to hire or buy their
friends; and masters, often from policy as well as from latent
humanity, allow those they are about to sell or let, to choose
their own places, if the persons they happen to select for masters
are considered safe *pay*. He promised to do all he could, and they
parted. But, every day, as long as the snow lasted, (for there was
snow on the ground at the time,) she returned to the spot where
they separated, and walking in the tracks her father had made in
the snow, repeated her prayer that "God would help her father
get her a new and better place."

A long time had not elapsed, when a fisherman by the name
of Scriver[6] appeared at Mr. Nealy's, and inquired of Isabel "if she
would like to go and live with him." She eagerly answered

"Yes," nothing doubting but he was sent in answer to her prayer; and she soon started off with him, walking while he rode; for he had bought her at the suggestion of her father, paying one hundred and five dollars for her. He also lived in Ulster County, but some five or six miles from Mr. Nealy's.

Scriver, besides being a fisherman, kept a tavern for the accommodation of people of his own class—for his was a rude, uneducated family, exceedingly profane in their language, but, on the whole, an honest, kind, and well-disposed people.

They owned a large farm, but left it wholly unimproved; attending mainly to their vocations of fishing and inn-keeping. Isabella declares she can ill describe the life she led with them. It was a wild, out-of-door kind of life. She was expected to carry fish, to hoe corn, to bring roots and herbs from the wood for beers, go to the Strand for a gallon of molasses or liquor as the case might require, and "browse around," as she expresses it. It was a life that suited her well for the time—being as devoid of hardship or terror as it was of improvement; a need which had not yet become a want. Instead of improving at this place, morally, she retrograded, as their example taught her to curse; and it was here that she took her first oath. After living with them about a year and a half, she was sold to one John J. Dumont, for the sum of seventy pounds. This was in 1810. Mr. Dumont lived in the same county as her former masters, in the town of New Paltz, and she remained with him till a short time previous to her emancipation by the State, in 1828.[7]

HER STANDING WITH HER NEW MASTER
AND MISTRESS

Had Mrs. Dumont possessed that vein of kindness and consideration for the slaves, so perceptible in her husband's character,

Isabella would have been as comfortable here, as one had *best* be, if one *must* be a slave. Mr. Dumont had been nursed in the very lap of slavery, and being naturally a man of kind feelings, treated his slaves with all the consideration he did his *other* animals, and *more,* perhaps. But Mrs. Dumont, who had been born and educated in a non-slaveholding family, and, like many others, used only to work-people, who, under the most stimulating of human motives, were willing to put forth their every energy, could not have patience with the creeping gait, the dull understanding, or see any cause for the listless manners and careless, slovenly habits of the poor down-trodden outcast—entirely forgetting that every high and efficient motive had been removed far from him; and that, had not his very intellect been crushed out of him, the slave would find little ground for aught but hopeless despondency. From this source arose a long series of trials in the life of our heroine, which we must pass over in silence; some, from motives of delicacy, and others, because the relation of them might inflict undeserved pain on some now living, whom Isabel remembers only with esteem and love; therefore, the reader will not be surprised if our narrative appear somewhat tame at this point, and may rest assured that it is not for want of facts, as the most thrilling incidents of this portion of her life are from various motives suppressed.

One comparatively trifling incident she wishes related, as it made a deep impression on her mind at the time—showing, as *she* thinks, how God shields the innocent, and causes them to triumph over their enemies, and also how she stood between master and mistress. In her family, Mrs. Dumont employed two white girls, one of whom, named Kate, evinced a disposition to "lord it over" Isabel, and, in her emphatic language "to *grind her down.*" Her master often shielded her from the attacks and accusations of others, praising her for her readiness and ability to work, and these praises seemed to foster a spirit of hostility to her, in the minds of Mrs. Dumont and her white servant, the latter of whom took every opportunity to cry up her faults, lessen her in the esteem of her master, and increase against her the displeasure of her mistress, which was already more than sufficient for Isabel's comfort. Her master insisted that she could do as much work as half-a-dozen common people, and do it well, too; whilst her mistress insisted that the first was true, only because it ever came from her hand but half performed. A good deal of feeling arose from this difference of opinion, which was getting to rather an uncomfortable height, when, all at once, the potatoes that Isabel cooked for breakfast assumed a dingy, dirty look. Her mistress blamed her severely, asking her master to observe "a fine specimen of Bell's work!"—adding, "it is the way *all* her work is done." Her master scolded also this time, and commanded her to be more careful in future. Kate joined with zest in the censures, and was very hard upon her. Isabella thought that she had done all she well could to have them nice; and became quite distressed at their appearances, and wondered what she should do to avoid them. In this dilemma, Gertrude Dumont (Mr. D.'s eldest child, a good, kind-hearted girl of ten years, who pitied Isabel sincerely), when she heard them all blame her so unsparingly, came forward, offering her sympathy and assistance; and when about to retire to bed, on the night of Isabella's humiliation, she advanced to Isabel, and told her, if she would wake her early next morning, she would get up and attend to her potatoes for her, while she (Isabella) went to milking, and they would see if they could not have them *nice,* and not have "Poppee," her word for father, and "Matty," her word for mother, and all of 'em, scolding so terribly.

Isabella gladly availed herself of this kindness, which touched her to the heart, amid so much of an opposite spirit. When Isabella had put the potatoes over to boil, Getty told her she would herself tend the fire, while Isabel milked. She had not long been seated by the fire, in performance of her promise, when Kate entered, and requested Gertrude to go out of the room and do something for her, which she refused, still keeping her place in the corner. While there, Kate came sweeping about the fire, caught up a chip, lifted some ashes with it, and dashed them into the kettle. Now the mystery was solved, the plot discovered! Kate was working a little too fast at making her mistress's words good, at showing that Mrs. Dumont and herself were on the right side of the dispute, and consequently at gaining power over Isabella. Yes, she was quite too fast, inasmuch as she had overlooked the little figure of justice, which sat in the corner, with scales nicely balanced, waiting to give all their dues.

But the time had come when she was to be overlooked no longer. It was Getty's turn to speak now. "Oh Poppee! oh Poppee!" said she, "Kate has been putting ashes in among the potatoes! I saw her do it! Look at those that fell on the outside of the kettle! You can now see what made the potatoes so dingy every morning, though Bell washed them clean!" And she repeated her story to every new comer, till the fraud was made as public as the censure of Isabella had been. Her mistress looked blank, and remained dumb—her master muttered something which sounded very like an oath—and poor Kate was so chopfallen, she looked like a convicted criminal, who would gladly have hid herself, (now that the baseness was out,) to conceal her mortified pride and deep chagrin.

It was a fine triumph for Isabella and her master, and she became more ambitious than ever to please him; and he stimulated her ambition by his commendation, and by boasting of her to his friends, telling them that *"that* wench" (pointing to Isabel) "is better to me than a *man*—for she will do a good family's washing in the night, and be ready in the morning to go into the field, where she will do as much at raking and binding as my best hands." Her ambition and desire to please were so great, that she often worked several nights in succession, sleeping only short snatches, as she sat in her chair; and some nights she would not allow herself to take any sleep, save what she could get resting herself against the wall, fearing that if she sat down, she would sleep too long. These extra exertions to please, and the praises consequent upon them, brought upon her head the envy of her fellow-slaves, and they taunted her with being the *"white folks' nigger."* On the other hand, she received the larger share of the confidence of her master, and many small favors that were by them unattainable. I asked her if her master, Dumont, ever whipped her? She answered, "Oh yes, he sometimes whipped me soundly, though never cruelly. And the most severe whipping he ever give me was because *I* was cruel to a cat." At this time she looked upon her master as a *God;* and believed that he knew of and could see her at all times, even as God himself. And she used sometimes to confess her delinquencies, from the conviction that he already knew them, and that she should fare better if she confessed voluntarily: and if any one talked to her of the injustice of her being a slave, she answered them with contempt, and immediately told her master. She then firmly believed that slavery was right and honorable. Yet she *now* sees very clearly the false position they were all in, both masters and slaves; and she looks back, with utter astonishment, at the absurdity of the claims so arrogantly set up by the masters, over beings designed by God to be as free as kings; and at the perfect stupidity of the slave, in admitting for one moment the validity of these claims.

In obedience to her mother's instructions, she had educated herself to such a sense of honesty, that, when she had become a mother, she would sometimes whip her child when it cried to her for bread, rather than give it a piece secretly, lest it should learn to take what was not its own! And the writer of this knows, from personal observation, that the slaveholders of the South feel it to be a *religious duty* to teach their slaves to be honest, and never to take what is not their own! Oh consistency, art thou not a jewel? Yet Isabella glories in the fact that she was faithful and true to her master; she says, "It made me true to my God"—

meaning, that it helped to form in her a character that loved truth, and hated a lie, and had saved her from the bitter pains and fears that are sure to follow in the wake of insincerity and hypocrisy.

As she advanced in years, an attachment sprung up between herself and a slave named Robert. But his master, an Englishman by the name of Catlin, anxious that no one's property but his own should be enhanced by the increase of his slaves, forbade Robert's visits to Isabella, and commanded him to take a wife among his fellow-servants. Notwithstanding this interdiction, Robert, following the bent of his inclinations, continued his visits to Isabel, though very stealthily, and, as he believed, without exciting the suspicion of his master; but one Saturday afternoon, hearing that Bell was ill, he took the liberty to go and see her. The first intimation *she* had of his visit was the appearance of her master, inquiring "if she had seen Bob." On her answering in the negative, he said to her, "If you see him, tell him to take care of himself, for the Catlins are after him." Almost at that instant, Bob made his appearance; and the first people he met were his old and his young masters. They were terribly enraged at finding him there, and the eldest began cursing, and calling upon his son to *"Knock down* the d——d black rascal"; at the same time, they both fell upon him like tigers, beating him with the heavy ends of their canes, bruising and mangling his head and face in the most awful manner, and causing the blood, which streamed from his wounds, to cover him like a slaughtered beast, constituting him a most shocking spectacle. Mr. Dumont interposed at this point, telling the ruffians they could no longer thus spill human blood on *his* premises—he would have "no niggers killed there." The Catlins then took a rope they had taken with them for the purpose, and tied Bob's hands behind him in such a manner, that Mr. Dumont insisted on loosening the cord, declaring that no brute should be tied in *that* manner, where *he* was. And as they led him away, like the greatest of criminals, the more humane Dumont followed them to their homes, as Robert's protector; and when he returned, he kindly went to Bell, as he called her, telling her he did not think they would strike him any more, as their wrath had greatly cooled before he left them. Isabella had witnessed this scene from her window, and was greatly shocked at the murderous treatment of poor Robert, whom she truly loved, and whose only crime, in the eye of his persecutors, was his affection for her. This beating, and we know not what after treatment, completely subdued the spirit of its victim, for Robert ventured no more to visit Isabella, but like an obedient and faithful chattel, took himself a wife from the house of his master. Robert did not live many years after his last visit to Isabel, but took his departure to that country, where "they neither marry nor are given in marriage," and where the oppressor cannot molest.

ISABELLA'S MARRIAGE

Subsequently, Isabella was married to a fellow-slave, named Thomas, who had previously had two wives, one of whom, if not both, had been torn from him and sold far away. And it is more than probable, that he was not only allowed but encouraged to take another at each successive sale. I say it is probable, because the writer of this knows from personal observation, that such is the custom among slaveholders at the present day; and that in a twenty months' residence among them, we never knew any one to open the lip against the practice; and when we severely censured it, the slaveholder had nothing to say; and the slave pleaded that, under existing circumstances, he could do no better.

Such an abominable state of things is silently tolerated, to say the least, by slaveholders—deny it who may. And what is that religion that sanctions, even by its silence, all that is embraced in the *"Peculiar Institution"*? If there *can* be any thing more diametrically opposed to the religion of Jesus, than the working of this soul-killing system—which is as truly sanctioned by the religion of America as are her ministers and churches—we wish to be shown where it can be found.

We have said, Isabella was married to Thomas—she was, after the fashion of slavery, one of the slaves performing the ceremony for them; as no true minister of Christ *can* perform, as in the presence of God, what he knows to be a mere *farce,* a *mock* marriage, unrecognised by any civil law, and liable to be annulled any moment, when the interest or caprice of the master should dictate.

With what feelings must slaveholders expect us to listen to their horror of amalgamation in prospect, while they are well aware that we know how calmly and quietly they contemplate the present state of licentiousness their own wicked laws have created, not only as it regards the slave, but as it regards the more privileged portion of the population of the South?

Slaveholders appear to me to take the same notice of the vices of the slave, as one does of the vicious disposition of his horse. They are often an inconvenience; further than that, they care not to trouble themselves about the matter.

ISABELLA AS A MOTHER

In process of time, Isabella found herself the mother of five children,[8] and she rejoiced in being permitted to be the instrument of increasing the property of her oppressors! Think, dear reader, without a blush, if you can, for one moment, of a *mother* thus willingly, and with *pride,* laying her own children, the "flesh of her flesh," on the altar of slavery—a sacrifice to the bloody

Moloch! But we must remember that beings capable of such sacrifices are not mothers; they are only "things," "chattels," "property."

But since that time, the subject of this narrative has made some advances from a state of chattelism towards that of a woman and a mother; and she now looks back upon her thoughts and feelings there, in her state of ignorance and degradation, as one does on the dark imagery of a fitful dream. One moment it seems but a frightful illusion; again it appears a terrible reality. I would to God it *were* but a dreamy myth, and not, as it now stands, a horrid reality to some three millions of chattelized human beings.

I have already alluded to her care not to teach her children to steal, by her example; and she says, with groanings that cannot be written, "The Lord only knows how many times I let my children go hungry, rather than take secretly the bread I liked not to ask for." All parents who annul their preceptive teachings by their daily practices would do well to profit by her example.

Another proof of her master's kindness of heart is found in the following fact. If her master came into the house and found her infant crying, (as she could not always attend to its wants and the commands of her mistress at the same time,) he would turn to his wife with a look of reproof, and ask her why she did not see the child taken care of; saying, most earnestly, "I will not hear this crying; I can't bear it, and I will not hear any child cry so. Here, Bell, take care of this child, if no more work is done for a week." And he would linger to see if his orders were obeyed, and not countermanded.

When Isabella went to the field to work, she used to put her infant in a basket, tying a rope to each handle, and suspending the basket to a branch of a tree, set another small child to swing it. It was thus secure from reptiles and was easily administered to, and even lulled to sleep, by a child too young for other labors. I was quite struck with the ingenuity of such a baby-tender, as

I have sometimes been with the swinging hammock the native mother prepares for her sick infant—apparently so much easier than aught we have in our more civilized homes; easier for the child, because it gets the motion without the least jar; and easier for the nurse, because the hammock is strung so high as to supersede the necessity of stooping.

SLAVEHOLDER'S PROMISES

After emancipation had been decreed by the State, some years before the time fixed for its consummation, Isabella's master told her if she would do well, and be faithful, he would give her "free papers," one year before she was legally free by statute. In the year 1826, she had a badly diseased hand, which greatly diminished her usefulness; but on the arrival of July 4, 1827, the time specified for her receiving her "free papers," she claimed the fulfilment of her master's promise; but he refused granting it, on account (as he alleged) of the loss he had sustained by her hand. She plead that she had worked all the time, and done many things she was not wholly able to do, although she knew she had been less useful than formerly; but her master remained inflexible. Her very faithfulness probably operated against her now, and he found it less easy than he thought to give up the profits of his faithful Bell, who had so long done him efficient service.

But Isabella inwardly determined that she would remain quietly with him only until she had spun his wool—about one hundred pounds—and then she would leave him, taking the rest of the time to herself. "Ah!" she says, with emphasis that cannot be written, "the slaveholders are TERRIBLE for promising to give you this or that, or such and such a privilege, if you will do thus and so; and when the time of fulfilment comes, and one claims the promise, they, forsooth, recollect nothing of the kind; and you are, like as not, taunted with being a LIAR; or, at best, the slave is accused of not having performed *his* part or condition of the contract. "Oh!" said she, "I have felt as if I could not live through the *operation* sometimes. Just think of us! *so* eager for our pleasures, and just foolish enough to keep feeding and feeding ourselves up with the idea that we should get what had been thus fairly promised; and when we think it is almost in our hands, find ourselves flatly denied! Just think! how *could* we bear it? Why, there was Charles Brodhead promised his slave Ned, that when harvesting was over, he might go and see his wife, who lived some twenty or thirty miles off. So Ned worked early and late, and as soon as the harvest was all in, he claimed the promised boon. His master said, he had merely told him he 'would *see* if he could go, when the harvest was over; but now he saw that he *could not* go.' But Ned, who still claimed a positive promise, on which he had fully depended, went on cleaning his shoes. His master asked him if he intended going, and on his replying 'yes,' took up a sled-stick that lay near him, and gave him such a blow on the head as broke his skull, killing him dead on the spot. The poor colored people all felt struck down by the blow." Ah! and well they might. Yet it was but one of a long series of bloody, and other most effectual blows, struck against their liberty and their lives.* But to return from our digression.

The subject of this narrative was to have been free July 4, 1827, but she continued with her master till the wool was spun, and the heaviest of the "fall's work" closed up, when she concluded to take her freedom into her own hands, and seek her fortune in some other place.

*Yet no official notice was taken of this more than brutal murder.

HER ESCAPE

The question in her mind, and one not easily solved, now was, "How can I get away?" So, as was her usual custom, she "told God she was afraid to go in the night, and in the day every body would see her." At length, the thought came to her that she could leave just before the day dawned, and get out of the neighborhood where she was known before the people were much astir. "Yes," said she, fervently, "that's a good thought! Thank you, God, for *that* thought!" So, receiving it as coming direct from God, she acted upon it, and one fine morning, a little before day-break, she might have been seen stepping stealthily away from the rear of Master Dumont's house, her infant on one arm and her wardrobe on the other; the bulk and weight of which, probably, she never found so convenient as on the present occasion, a cotton handkerchief containing both her clothes and her provisions.

As she gained the summit of a high hill, a considerable distance from her master's, the sun offended her by coming forth in all his pristine splendor. She thought it never was so light before; indeed, she thought it much too light. She stopped to look about her, and ascertain if her pursuers were yet in sight. No one appeared, and, for the first time, the question came up for settlement, "Where, and to whom, shall I go?" In all her thoughts of getting away, she had not once asked herself whither she should direct her steps. She sat down, fed her infant, and again turning her thoughts to God, her only help, she prayed him to direct her to some safe asylum. And soon it occurred to her, that there was a man living somewhere in the direction she had been pursuing, by the name of Levi Rowe, whom she had known, and who, she thought, would be likely to befriend her. She accordingly pursued her way to his house, where she

the express understanding, that he was soon to return to the State of New York, and be emancipated at the specified time.[11]

When Isabel heard that her son had been sold South, she immediately started on foot and alone, to find the man who had thus dared, in the face of all law, human and divine, to sell her child out of the State; and if possible, to bring him to account for the deed.

Arriving at New Paltz, she went directly to her former mistress, Dumont, complaining bitterly of the removal of her son. Her mistress heard her through, and then replied—*"Ugh! a fine fuss to make about a little nigger! Why, haven't you as many of 'em left as you can see to, and take care of? A pity 'tis, the niggers are not all in Guinea! ! Making such a halloo-balloo about the neighborhood; and all for a paltry nigger! ! !"* Isabella heard her through, and after a moment's hesitation, answered, in tones of deep determination—*"I'll have my child again."* "Have *your child* again!" repeated her mistress—her tones big with contempt, and scorning the absurd idea of her getting him. "How can you get him? And what have you to support him with, if you could? Have you any money?" "No," answered Bell, "I have no money, but God has enough, or what's better! And I'll have my child again." These words were pronounced in the most slow, solemn, and determined measure and manner. And in speaking of it, she says, "Oh my God! I know'd I'd have him agin. I was sure God would help me to get him. Why, I felt so *tall within*—I felt as if the *power of a nation* was with me!"

The impressions made by Isabella on her auditors, when moved by lofty or deep feeling, can never be transmitted to paper, (to use the words of another,) till by some Daguerrian act, we are enabled to transfer the look, the gesture, the tones of voice, in connection with the quaint, yet fit expressions used, and the spirit-stirring animation that, at such a time, pervades all she says.

After leaving her mistress, she called on Mrs. Gedney, mother
of him who had sold her boy; who, after listening to her lamentations, her grief being mingled with indignation at the sale of
her son, and her declaration that she would have him again—
said, "Dear me! What a disturbance to make about your child!
What is *your* child, better than *my* child? My child is gone out
there, and yours is gone to live with her, to have enough of
every thing, and be treated like a gentleman!" And here she
laughed at Isabel's absurd fears, as she would represent them to
be. "Yes," said Isabel, *"your* child has gone there, but she is
married, and my boy has gone as a *slave!* and he is too little to go
so far from his mother. Oh, I must have my child." And here the
continued laugh of Mrs. G. seemed to Isabel, in this time of
anguish and distress, almost demoniacal. And well it was for Mrs.
Gedney, that, at that time, she could not even dream of the
awful fate awaiting her own beloved daughter, at the hands of
him whom she had chosen as worthy the wealth of her love
and confidence, and in whose society her young heart had
calculated on a happiness, purer and more elevated than was ever
conferred by a kingly crown. But, alas! she was doomed to
disappointment, as we shall relate by and by. At this point,
Isabella earnestly begged of God that he would show to those
about her that he was her helper; and she adds, in narrating,
"And he *did;* or, if he did not show them, he did me."

IT IS OFTEN DARKEST, JUST BEFORE DAWN

This homely proverb was illustrated in the case of our sufferer;
for, at the period at which we have arrived in our narrative, to
her the darkness seemed palpable, and the waters of affliction
covered her soul; yet light was about to break in upon her.

Soon after the scenes related in our last chapter, which had harrowed up her very soul to agony, she met a man, (we would like to tell you *who,* dear reader, but it would be doing him no kindness, even at the present day, to do so,) who evidently sympathized with her, and counselled her to go to the Quakers, telling her they were already feeling very indignant at the fraudulent sale of her son, and assuring her that they would readily assist her, and direct her what to do. He pointed out to her two houses, where lived some of those people, who formerly, more than any other sect, perhaps, lived out the principles of the gospel of Christ. She wended her way to their dwellings, was listened to, unknown as she personally was to them, with patience, and soon gained their sympathies and active coöperation.

They gave her lodgings for the night; and it is very amusing to hear her tell of the "nice, high, clean, white, *beautiful* bed" assigned her to sleep in, which contrasted so strangely with her former pallets, that she sat down and contemplated it, perfectly absorbed in wonder that *such* a bed should have been appropriated to one like herself. For some time she thought that she would lie down beneath it, on her usual bedstead, the floor. "I did indeed," says she, laughing heartily at her former self. However, she finally concluded to make use of the bed, for fear that not to do so might injure the feelings of her good hostess. In the morning, the Quaker saw that she was taken and set down near Kingston, with directions to go to the Court House, and enter complaint to the grand jury.

By a little inquiry, she found which was the building she sought, went into the door, and taking the first man she saw of imposing appearance for the *grand* jury, she commenced her complaint. But he very civilly informed her there was no grand jury there; she must go up stairs. When she had with some difficulty ascended the flight through the crowd that filled them, she again turned to the *"grandest"* looking man she could select, telling him she had come to enter a complaint to the grand jury. For his own amusement, he inquired what her complaint was;

but, when he saw it was a serious matter, he said to her, "This is no place to enter a complaint—go in there," pointing in a particular direction.

She then went in, where she found the Grand Jurors indeed sitting, and again commenced to relate her injuries. After holding some conversation among themselves, one of them rose, and bidding her follow him, led the way to a side office, where he heard her story, and asked her "if she could *swear* that the child she spoke of was her son?" "Yes," she answered, "I *swear* it's my son." "Stop, stop!" said the lawyer, "you must swear by this book"—giving her a book, which she thinks must have been the Bible. She took it, and putting it to her lips, began again to swear it was her child. The clerks, unable to preserve their gravity any longer, burst into an uproarious laugh; and one of them inquired of lawyer Chip[12] of what use it could be to make *her* swear. "It will answer the law," replied the officer. He then made her comprehend just what he wished her to do, and she took a lawful oath, as far as the outward ceremony could make it one. All can judge how far she understood its spirit and meaning.

He now gave her a writ, directing her to take it to the constable at New Paltz, and have him serve it on Solomon Gedney. She obeyed, walking, or rather *trotting,* in her haste, some eight or nine miles.

But while the constable, through mistake, served the writ on a brother of the real culprit, Solomon Gedney slipped into a boat, and was nearly across the North River, on whose banks they were standing, before the dull Dutch constable was aware of his mistake. Solomon Gedney, meanwhile, consulted a lawyer, who advised him to go to Alabama and bring back the boy, otherwise it might cost him fourteen years' imprisonment, and a thousand dollars in cash. By this time, it is hoped he began to feel that selling slaves unlawfully was not so good a business as he had wished to find it. He secreted himself till due preparations could be made, and soon set sail for Alabama. Steamboats and railroads had not then annihilated distance to the extent they now have, and although he left in the fall of the year, spring came ere he returned, bringing the boy with him—but holding on to him as his property. It had ever been Isabella's prayer, not only that her son might be returned, but that he should be delivered from bondage, and into her own hands, lest he should be punished out of mere spite to her, who was so greatly annoying and irritating to her oppressors; and if her suit was gained, her very triumph would add vastly to their irritation.

She again sought advice of Esquire Chip, whose counsel was, that the aforesaid constable serve the before-mentioned writ upon the right person. This being done, soon brought Solomon Gedney up to Kingston, where he gave bonds for his appearance at court, in the sum of $600.

Esquire Chip next informed his client, that her case must now lie over till the next session of the court, some months in the future. "The law must take its course," said he.

"What! wait another court! wait *months?*" said the persevering mother. "Why, long before that time, he can go clear off, and take my child with him—no one knows where. I *cannot* wait; I *must* have him *now,* whilst he is to be had." "Well," said the lawyer, very coolly, "if he puts the boy out of the way, he must pay the $600—one half of which will be yours"; supposing, perhaps, that $300 would pay for a "heap of children," in the eye of a slave who never, in all her life, called a dollar her own. But in this instance, he was mistaken in his reckoning. She assured him, that she had not been seeking money, neither would money satisfy her; it was her son, and her son alone she wanted, and her son she must have. Neither could she wait court, not she. The lawyer used his every argument to convince her, that she ought to be very thankful for what they had done for her; that it was a great deal, and it was but reasonable that she should now wait patiently the time of the court.

Yet she never felt, for a moment, like being influenced by

these suggestions. She felt confident she was to receive a full and
literal answer to her prayer, the burden of which had been—"O
Lord, give my son into my hands, and that speedily! Let not the
spoilers have him any longer." Notwithstanding, she very distinctly saw that those who had thus far helped her on so kindly
were *wearied* of her, and she feared God was wearied also. She had
a short time previous learned that Jesus was a Savior, and an
intercessor; and she thought that if Jesus could be induced to plead
for her in the present trial, God would listen to *him,* though he
were wearied of *her* importunities. To him, of course, she applied.
As she was walking about, scarcely knowing whither she went,
asking within herself, "Who will show me any good, and lend a
helping hand in this matter," she was accosted by a perfect
stranger, and one whose name she has never learned, in the
following terms: "Halloo, there; how do you get along with your
boy? do they give him up to you?" She told him all, adding that
now every body was tired, and she had none to help her. He said,
"Look here! I'll tell you what you'd better do. Do you see that
stone house yonder?" pointing in a particular direction. "Well,
lawyer Demain[13] lives there, and do you go to him, and lay your
case before him; I think he'll help you. *Stick to him*. Don't give him
peace till he does. I feel sure if you press him, he'll do it for you."
She needed no further urging, but trotted off at her peculiar gait in
the direction of his house, as fast as possible,—and she was not
encumbered with stockings, shoes, or any other heavy article of
dress. When she had told him her story, in her impassioned
manner, he looked at her a few moments, as if to ascertain if he
were contemplating a new variety of the genus homo, and then
told her, if she would give him five dollars, he would get her son
for her, in twenty-four hours. "Why," she replied, *"I have no
money,* and never had a dollar in my life!" Said he, "If you will go
to those Quakers in Poppletown, who carried you to court, they
will help you to five dollars in cash, I have no doubt; and you shall
have your son in twenty-four hours, from the time you bring me

that sum." She performed the journey to Poppletown, a distance of some ten miles, very expeditiously; collected considerable more than the sum specified by the barrister; then, shutting the money tightly in her hand, she trotted back, and paid the lawyer a larger fee than he had demanded. When inquired of by people what she had done with the overplus, she answered, "Oh, I got it for lawyer Demain, and I gave it to him." They assured her she was a *fool* to do so; that she should have kept all over five dollars, and purchased herself shoes with it. "Oh, I do not want money or clothes now, I only want my son; and if five dollars will get him, more will *surely* get him." And if the lawyer had returned it to her, she avers she would not have accepted it. She was perfectly willing he should have every coin she could raise, if he would but restore her lost son to her. Moreover, the five dollars he required were for the remuneration of him who should go after her son and his master, and not for his own services.

The lawyer now renewed his promise, that she should have her son in twenty-four hours. But Isabella, having no idea of this space of time, went several times in a day, to ascertain if her son had come. Once, when the servant opened the door and saw her, she said, in a tone expressive of much surprise, "Why, this woman's come again!" She then wondered if she went too often. When the lawyer appeared, he told her the twenty-four hours would not expire until the next morning; if she would call then, she would see her son. The next morning saw Isabel at the lawyer's door, while he was yet in his bed. He now assured her it was morning till noon; and that before noon her son would be there, for he had sent the famous "Matty Styles" after him, who would not fail to have the boy and his master on hand in due season, either dead or alive; of that he was sure. Telling her she need not come again; he would himself inform her of their arrival.

After dinner, he appeared at Mr. Rutzer's, (a place the lawyer had procured for her, while she awaited the arrival of her boy,) assuring her, her son had come; but that he stoutly denied having any mother, or any relatives in that place; and said, "she must go over and identify him." She went to the office, but at sight of her the boy cried aloud, and regarded her as some terrible being, who was about to take him away from a kind and loving friend. He knelt, even, and begged them, with tears, not to take him away from his dear master, who had brought him from the dreadful South, and been so kind to him.

When he was questioned relative to the bad scar on his forehead, he said, "Fowler's horse hove him." And of the one on his cheek, "That was done by running against the carriage." In answering these questions, he looked imploringly at his master, as much as to say, "If they are falsehoods, you bade me say them; may they be satisfactory to you, at least."

The justice, noting his appearance, bade him forget his master and attend only to him. But the boy persisted in denying his mother, and clinging to his master, saying his mother did not live in such a place as that. However, they allowed the mother to identify her son; and Esquire Demain pleaded that he claimed the boy for her, on the ground that he had been sold out of the State, contrary to the laws in such cases made and provided— spoke of the penalties annexed to said crime, and of the sum of money the delinquent was to pay, in case any one chose to prosecute him for the offence he had committed. Isabella, who was sitting in a corner, scarcely daring to breathe, thought within herself, "If I can but get the boy, the $200 may remain for whoever else chooses to prosecute—*I* have done enough to make myself enemies already"—and she trembled at the thought of the formidable enemies she had probably arrayed against herself—helpless and despised as she was. When the pleading was at an end, Isabella understood the Judge[14] to declare, as the sentence of the Court, that the "boy be delivered into the hands of the mother—having no other master, no other controller, no other conductor, but his mother." This sentence was obeyed; he was delivered into her hands, the boy meanwhile begging, most piteously, *not* to be taken from his dear master, saying she was not his mother, and that his mother did not live in such a place as that. And it was some time before lawyer Demain, the clerks, and Isabella, could collectively succeed in calming the child's fears, and in convincing him that Isabella was not some terrible monster, as he had for the last months, probably, been trained to believe; and who, in taking him away from his master, was taking him from all good, and consigning him to all evil.

When at last kind words and *bon-bons* had quieted his fears, and he could listen to their explanations, he said to Isabella— "Well, you *do* look like my mother *used* to"; and she was soon able to make him comprehend some of the obligations he was under, and the relation he stood in, both to herself and his master. She commenced as soon as practicable to examine the boy, and found, to her utter astonishment, that from the crown of his head to the sole of his foot, the callosities and indurations on his entire body were most frightful to behold. His back she described as being like her fingers, as she laid them side by side.

"Heavens! what is all *this*?" said Isabel. He answered, "It is where Fowler whipped, kicked, and beat me." She exclaimed, "Oh, Lord Jesus, look! see my poor child! Oh Lord, 'render unto them double' for all this! Oh my God! Pete, how *did* you bear it?"

"Oh, this is nothing, mammy—if you should see Phillis, I guess you'd *scare!* She had a little baby, and Fowler cut her till the milk as well as blood ran down *her* body. You would *scare* to see Phillis, mammy."

When Isabella inquired, "What did Miss Eliza★ say, Pete, when you were treated so badly?" he replied, "Oh, mammy, she said she wished I was with Bell. Sometimes I crawled under the stoop, mammy, the blood running all about me, and my back

★Meaning Mrs. Eliza Fowler.

would stick to the boards; and sometimes Miss Eliza would come and grease my sores, when all were abed and asleep."

DEATH OF MRS. ELIZA FOWLER

As soon as possible, she procured a place for Peter, as tender of Locks, at a place called Wahkendall, near Greenkills. After he was thus disposed of, she visited her sister Sophia, who resided at Newberg, and spent the winter in several different families where she was acquainted. She remained sometimes in the family of a Mr. Latin, who was a relative of Solomon Gedney; and the latter, when he found Isabel with his cousin, used all his influence to persuade him she was a great mischief-maker and a very troublesome person,—that she had put him to some hundreds of dollars expense, by fabricating lies about him, and especially his sister and her family, concerning her boy, when the latter was living so like a gentleman with them; and, for his part, he would not advise his friends to harbor or encourage her. However, his cousins, the Latins, could not see with the eyes of *his* feelings, and consequently his words fell powerless on them, and they retained her in their service as long as they had aught for her to do.

She then went to visit her former master, Dumont. She had scarcely arrived there, when Mr. Fred. Waring entered, and seeing Isabel, pleasantly accosted her, and asked her "what she was driving at now-a-days." On her answering "nothing particular," he requested her to go over to his place, and assist his folks, as some of them were sick, and they needed an extra hand. She very gladly assented. When Mr. W. retired, her master wanted to know why she wished to help people, that called her the "worst of devils," as Mr. Waring had done in the courthouse—for he was the uncle of Solomon Gedney, and attended the trial we have described—and declared "that she was a *fool* to; *he* wouldn't do it." "Oh," she told him, "she would not mind that, but was very glad to have people forget their anger towards her." She went over, but too happy to feel that their resentment was passed, and commenced her work with a light heart and a strong will. She had not worked long in this frame of mind, before a young daughter of Mr. Waring rushed into the rooms exclaiming, with uplifted hands—"Heavens and earth, Isabella! Fowler's murdered Cousin Eliza!" "Ho," said Isabel, *"that's* nothing—he liked to have killed *my* child; nothing saved him but God." Meaning, that she was not at all surprised at it, for a man whose heart was sufficiently hardened to treat a mere child as hers had been treated, was, in her opinion, more fiend than human, and prepared for the commission of any crime that his passions might prompt him to. The child further informed her that a letter had arrived by mail bringing the news.

Immediately after this announcement, Solomon Gedney and his mother came in, going direct to Mrs. Waring's room, where she soon heard tones as of some one reading. She thought something said to her inwardly, "Go up stairs and hear." At first she hesitated, but it seemed to press her the more—"Go up and hear!" She went up, unusual as it is for slaves to leave their work and enter unbidden their mistress's room, for the sole purpose of seeing or hearing what may be seen or heard there. But on this occasion, Isabella says, she walked in at the door, shut it, placed her back against it, and listened. She saw them and heard them read—"He knocked her down with his fist, jumped on her with his knees, broke her collar-bone, and tore out her wind-pipe! He then attempted his escape, but was pursued and arrested, and put in an iron bank for safe-keeping!" And the friends were requested to go down and take away the poor innocent children who had thus been made in one short day more than orphans.

If this narrative should ever meet the eye of those innocent sufferers for another's guilt, let them not be too deeply affected

by the relation; but, placing their confidence in Him who sees
the end from the beginning, and controls the results, rest secure
in the faith, that, although they may physically suffer for the sins
of others, if they remain but true to themselves, their highest and
more enduring interests can never suffer from such a cause. This
relation should be suppressed for their sakes, were it not even
now so often denied, that slavery is fast undermining all true
regard for human life. We know this one instance is not a
demonstration to the contrary; but, adding this to the lists of
tragedies that weekly come up to us through the Southern mails,
may we not admit them as proofs irrefragable? The newspapers
confirmed this account of the terrible affair.

When Isabella had heard the letter, all being too much absorbed in their own feelings to take note of her, she returned to
her work, her heart swelling with conflicting emotions. She was
awed at the dreadful deed; she mourned the fate of the loved
Eliza, who had in such an undeserved and barbarous manner
been put away from her labors and watchings as a tender mother;
and, "last though not least," in the development of her character
and spirit, her heart bled for the afflicted relatives; even those of
them who "laughed at her calamity, and mocked when her fear
came." Her thoughts dwelt long and intently on the subject, and
the wonderful chain of events that had conspired to bring her
that day to that house, to listen to that piece of intelligence—
to that house, where she never was before or afterwards in her
life, and invited there by people who had so lately been hotly
incensed against her. It all seemed very remarkable to her, and
she viewed it as flowing from a special providence of God. She
thought she saw clearly, that their unnatural bereavement was a
blow dealt in retributive justice; but she found it not in her heart
to exult or rejoice over them. She felt as if God had more than
answered her petition, when she ejaculated, in her anguish of
mind, "Oh, Lord, render unto them double!" She said, "I dared
not find fault with God, exactly; but the language of my heart

was, "Oh, my God! that's too much—I did not mean quite so much, God!" It was a terrible blow to the friends of the deceased; and her selfish mother (who, said Isabella, made such a "to-do about *her* boy, not from affection, but to have her own will and way") went deranged, and walking to and fro in her delirium, called aloud for her poor murdered daughter—*"Eliza! Eliza!"*

The derangement of Mrs. G. was a matter of hearsay, as Isabella saw her not after the trial; but she has no reason to doubt the truth of what she heard. Isabel could never learn the subsequent fate of Fowler, but heard, in the spring of '49, that his children had been seen in Kingston—one of whom was spoken of as a fine, interesting girl, albeit a halo of sadness fell like a veil about her.

ISABELLA'S RELIGIOUS EXPERIENCE

We will now turn from the outward and temporal to the inward and spiritual life of our subject. It is ever both interesting and instructive to trace the exercises of a human mind, through the trials and mysteries of life; and especially a naturally powerful mind, left as hers was almost entirely to its own workings, and the chance influences it met on its way; and especially to note its reception of that divine "light, that lighteth every man that cometh into the world."

We see, as knowledge dawns upon it, truth and error strangely commingled; here, a bright spot illuminated by truth—and there, one darkened and distorted by error; and the state of such a soul may be compared to a landscape at early dawn, where the sun is seen superbly gilding some objects, and causing others to send forth their lengthened, distorted, and sometimes hideous shadows.

Her mother, as we have already said, talked to her of God. From these conversations, her incipient mind drew the conclusion, that God was "a great man"; greatly superior to other men in power; and being located "high in the sky," could see all that transpired on the earth. She believed he not only saw, but noted down all her actions in a great book, even as her master kept a record of whatever he wished not to forget. But she had no idea that God knew a thought of hers till she had uttered it aloud.

As we have before mentioned, she had ever been mindful of her mother's injunctions, spreading out in detail all her troubles before God, imploring and firmly trusting him to send her deliverance from them. Whilst yet a child, she listened to a story of a wounded soldier, left alone in the trail of a flying army, helpless and starving, who hardened the very ground about him with kneeling in his supplications to God for relief, until it arrived. From this narrative, she was deeply impressed with the idea, that if *she* also were to present her petitions under the open canopy of heaven, speaking very loud, she should the more readily be heard; consequently, she sought a fitting spot for this, her rural sanctuary. The place she selected, in which to offer up her daily orisons, was a small island in a small stream, covered with large willow shrubbery, beneath which the sheep had made their pleasant winding paths; and sheltering themselves from the scorching rays of a noon-tide sun, luxuriated in the cool shadows of the graceful willows, as they listened to the tiny falls of the silver waters. It was a lonely spot, and chosen by her for its beauty, its retirement, and because she thought that there, in the noise of those waters, she could speak louder to God, without being overheard by any who might pass that way. When she had made choice of her sanctum, at a point of the island where the stream met, after having been separated, she improved it by pulling away the branches of the shrubs from the centre, and weaving them together for a wall on the outside, forming a circular arched alcove, made entirely of the graceful willow. To this place she resorted daily, and in pressing times much more frequently.

At this time, her prayers, or, more appropriately, "talks with God," were perfectly original and unique, and would be well worth preserving, were it possible to give the tones and manner with the words; but no adequate idea of them can be written while the tones and manner remain inexpressible.

She would sometimes repeat, "Our Father in heaven," in her Low Dutch, as taught her by her mother; after that, all was from the suggestions of her own rude mind. She related to God, in minute detail, all her troubles and sufferings, inquiring, as she proceeded, "Do you think that's right, God?" and closed by begging to be delivered from the evil, whatever it might be.

She talked to God as familiarly as if he had been a creature like herself; and a thousand times more so, than if she had been in the presence of some earthly potentate. She demanded, with little expenditure of reverence or fear, a supply of all her more pressing wants, and at times her demands approached very near to commands. She felt as if God was under obligation to her, much more than she was to him. He seemed to her benighted vision in some manner bound to do her bidding.

Her heart recoils now, with very dread, when she recalls those shocking, almost blasphemous conversations with great Jehovah. And well for herself did she deem it, that, unlike earthly potentates, his infinite character combined the tender father with the omniscient and omnipotent Creator of the universe.

She at first commenced promising God, that if he would help her out of all her difficulties, she would pay him by being very good; and this goodness she intended as a remuneration to God. She could think of no benefit that was to accrue to herself or her fellow-creatures, from her leading a life of purity and generous self-sacrifice for the good of others; as far as any but God was

concerned, she saw nothing in it but heart-trying penance, sustained by the sternest exertion; and this she soon found much
more easily promised than performed.

Days wore away—new trials came—God's aid was invoked,
and the same promises repeated; and every successive night
found her part of the contract unfulfilled. She now began to
excuse herself, by telling God she could not be good in her
present circumstances; but if he would give her a new place, and
a good master and mistress, she could and would be good; and
she expressly stipulated, that she would be good *one* day to show
God how good she would be *all* of the time, when he should
surround her with the right influences, and she should be delivered from the temptations that then so sorely beset her. But, alas!
when night came, and she became conscious that she had yielded
to all her temptations, and entirely failed of keeping her word
with God, having prayed and promised one hour, and fallen into
the sins of anger and profanity the next, the mortifying reflection
weighed on her mind, and blunted her enjoyment. Still, she did
not lay it deeply to heart, but continued to repeat her demands
for aid, and her promises of pay, with full purpose of heart, at
each particular time, that *that* day she would not fail to keep her
plighted word.

Thus perished the inward spark, like a flame just igniting,
when one waits to see whether it will burn on or die out, till the
long desired change came, and she found herself in a new place,
with a good mistress, and one who never instigated an otherwise
kind master to be unkind to her; in short, a place where she had
literally nothing to complain of, and where, for a time, she was
more happy than she could well express. "Oh, every thing there
was *so* pleasant, and kind, and good, and all so comfortable;
enough of every thing; indeed, it was beautiful!" she exclaimed.

Here, at Mr. Van Wagener's,—as the reader will readily
perceive she must have been,—she was so happy and satisfied,
that God was entirely forgotten. Why should her thoughts turn

to him, who was only known to her as a help in trouble? She had no trouble now; her every prayer had been answered in every minute particular. She had been delivered from her persecutors and temptations, her youngest child had been given her, and the others she knew she had no means of sustaining if she had them with her, and was content to leave them behind. Their father, who was much older than Isabel, and who preferred serving his time out in slavery, to the trouble and dangers of the course she pursued, remained with and could keep an eye on them—though it is comparatively little that they can do for each other while they remain in slavery; and this little the slave, like persons in every other situation of life, is not always disposed to perform. There *are* slaves, who, copying the selfishness of their superiors in power, in their conduct towards their fellows who may be thrown upon their mercy, by infirmity or illness, allow them to suffer for want of that kindness and care which it is fully in their power to render them.

The slaves in this country have ever been allowed to celebrate the principal, if not some of the lesser festivals observed by the Catholics and Church of England;—many of them not being required to do the least service for several days, and at Christmas they have almost universally an entire week to themselves, except, perhaps, the attending to a few duties, which are absolutely required for the comfort of the families they belong to. If much service is desired, they are hired to do it, and paid for it as if they were free. The more sober portion of them spend these holidays in earning a little money. Most of them visit and attend parties and balls, and not a few of them spend it in the lowest dissipation. This respite from toil is granted them by all religionists, of whatever persuasion, and probably originated from the fact that many of the first slaveholders were members of the Church of England.

Frederick Douglass, who has devoted his great heart and noble talents entirely to the furtherance of the cause of his

down-trodden race, has said—"From what I know of the effect
of their holidays upon the slave, I believe them to be among the
most effective means, in the hands of the slaveholder, in keeping
down the spirit of insurrection. Were the slaveholders at once to
abandon this practice, I have not the slightest doubt it would
lead to an immediate insurrection among the slaves. These holidays serve as conductors, or safety-valves, to carry off the rebellious spirit of enslaved humanity. But for these, the slave would
be forced up to the wildest desperation; and woe betide the
slaveholder, the day he ventures to remove or hinder the operation of those conductors! I warn him that, in such an event, a
spirit will go forth in their midst, more to be dreaded than the
most appalling earthquake."

When Isabella had been at Mr. Van Wagener's a few months,
she saw in prospect one of the festivals approaching. She knows
it by none but the Dutch name, Pingster,[15] as she calls it—but
I think it must have been Whitsuntide, in English. She says she
"looked back into Egypt," and every thing looked "so pleasant
there," as she saw retrospectively all her former companions
enjoying their freedom for at least a little space, as well as their
wonted convivialities, and in her heart she longed to be with
them. With this picture before her mind's eye, she contrasted the
quiet, peaceful life she was living with the excellent people of
Wahkendall, and it seemed so dull and void of incident, that the
very contrast served but to heighten her desire to return, that, at
least, she might enjoy with them, once more, the coming festivi-
ties. These feelings had occupied a secret corner of her breast for
some time, when, one morning, she told Mrs. Van Wagener that
her old master Dumont would come that day, and that she
should go home with him on his return. They expressed some
surprise, and asked her where she obtained her information. She
replied, that no one had told her, but she felt that he would
come.

It seemed to have been one of those "events that cast their

shadows before"; for, before night, Mr. Dumont made his appearance. She informed him of her intention to accompany him home. He answered, with a smile, "I shall not take you back again; you ran away from me." Thinking his manner contradicted his words, she did not feel repulsed, but made herself and child ready; and when her former master had seated himself in the open dearborn, she walked towards it, intending to place herself and child in the rear, and go with him. But, ere she reached the vehicle, she says that God revealed himself to her, with all the suddenness of a flash of lightning, showing her, "in the twinkling of an eye, that he was *all over*"—that he pervaded the universe—"and that there was no place where God was not." She became instantly conscious of her great sin in forgetting her almighty Friend and "ever-present help in time of trouble." All her unfulfilled promises arose before her, like a vexed sea whose waves run mountains high; and her soul, which seemed but one mass of lies, shrunk back aghast from the "awful look" of him whom she had formerly talked to, as if he had been a being like herself; and she would now fain have hid herself in the bowels of the earth, to have escaped his dread presence. But she plainly saw there was no place, not even in hell, where he was not; and where could she flee? Another such "a look," as she expressed it, and she felt that she must be extinguished forever, even as one, with the breath of his mouth, "blows out a lamp," so that no spark remains.

A dire dread of annihilation now seized her, and she waited to see if, by "another look," she was to be stricken from existence,—swallowed up, even as the fire licketh up the oil with which it comes in contact.

When at last the second look came not, and her attention was once more called to outward things, she observed her master had left, and exclaiming aloud, "Oh, God, I did not know you were so big," walked into the house, and made an effort to resume her work. But the workings of the inward man were too absorbing to admit of much attention to her avocations. She desired to talk to God, but her vileness utterly forbade it, and she was not able to prefer a petition. "What!" said she, "shall I lie again to God? I have told him nothing but lies; and shall I speak again, and tell another lie to God?" She could not; and now she began to wish for some one to speak to God for her. Then a space seemed opening between her and God, and she felt that if some one, who was worthy in the sight of heaven, would but plead *for* her in their own name, and not let God know it came from *her,* who was so unworthy, God might grant it. At length a friend appeared to stand between herself and an insulted Deity; and she felt as sensibly refreshed as when, on a hot day, an umbrella had been interposed between her scorching head and a burning sun. But who was this friend? became the next inquiry. Was it Deencia, who had so often befriended her? She looked at her, with her new power of sight—and, lo! she, too, seemed all "bruises and putrifying sores," like herself. No, it was some one very different from Deencia.

"Who *are* you?" she exclaimed, as the vision brightened into a form distinct, beaming with the beauty of holiness, and radiant with love. She then said, audibly addressing the mysterious visitant—"I *know* you, and I *don't* know you." Meaning, "You seem perfectly familiar; I feel that you not only love me, but that you always *have* loved me—yet I know you not—I cannot call you by name." When she said, "I know you," the subject of the vision remained distinct and quiet. When she said, "I don't know you," it moved restlessly about, like agitated waters. So while she repeated, without intermission, "I know you, I know you," that the vision might remain—"Who are you?" was the cry of her heart, and her whole soul was in one deep prayer that this heavenly personage might be revealed to her, and remain with her. At length, after bending both soul and body with the intensity of this desire, till breath and strength seemed failing, and she could maintain her position no longer, an answer came to her, saying distinctly, "It is Jesus." "Yes," she responded, "it is *Jesus*."

Previous to these exercises of mind, she heard Jesus mentioned in reading or speaking, but had received from what she heard no impression that he was any other than an eminent man, like a Washington or a Lafayette. Now he appeared to her delighted mental vision as so mild, so good, and so every way lovely, and he loved her so much! And, how strange that he had always loved her, and she had never known it! And how great a blessing he conferred, in that he should stand between her and God! And God was no longer a terror and a dread to her.

She stopped not to argue the point, even in her own mind, whether he had reconciled her to God, or God to herself, (though she thinks the former now,) being but too happy that God was no longer to her as a consuming fire, and Jesus was "altogether lovely." Her heart was now full of joy and gladness, as it had been of terror, and at one time of despair. In the light of her great happiness, the world was clad in new beauty, the very air sparkled as with diamonds, and was redolent of heaven. She contemplated the unapproachable barriers that existed between herself and the great of this world, as the world calls greatness, and made surprising comparisons between them, and the union existing between herself and Jesus,—Jesus, the transcendently lovely, as well as great and powerful; for so he appeared to her, though he seemed but human; and she watched for his bodily appearance, feeling that she should know him, if she saw him; and when he came, she should go and dwell with him, as with a dear friend.

It was not given her to see that he loved any other; and she thought if others came to know and love him, as she did, she should be thrust aside and forgotten, being herself but a poor ignorant slave, with little to recommend her to his notice. And when she heard him spoken of, she said mentally—"What! others know Jesus? I thought no one knew Jesus but me!" and she felt a sort of jealousy, lest she should be robbed of her newly found treasure.

She conceived, one day, as she listened to reading, that she heard an intimation that Jesus was married, and hastily inquired if Jesus had a wife. "What!" said the reader, "*God* have a wife?" "Is Jesus *God*?" inquired Isabella. "Yes, to be sure he is," was the answer returned. From this time, her conceptions of Jesus became more elevated and spiritual; and she sometimes spoke of him as God, in accordance with the teaching she had received.

But when she was simply told, that the Christian world was much divided on the subject of Christ's nature—some believing him to be coëqual with the Father—to be God in and of himself, "very God, of very God";—some, that he is the "well-beloved," "only begotten Son of God";—and others, that he is, or was, rather, but a mere man—she said, "Of that I only know as I saw. I did not see him to be God; else, how could he stand between me and God? I saw him as a friend, standing between me and God, through whom, love flowed as from a fountain." Now, so far from expressing her views of Christ's character and office in accordance with any system of theology extant, she says she believes Jesus is the same spirit that was in our first parents, Adam and Eve, in the beginning, when they came from the hand of their Creator. When they sinned through disobedience, this pure spirit forsook them, and fled to heaven; that there it remained, until it returned again in the person of Jesus; and that, previous to a personal union with him, man is but a brute, possessing only the spirit of an animal.

She avers that, in her darkest hours, she had no fear of any worse hell than the one she then carried in her bosom; though it had ever been pictured to her in its deepest colors, and threatened her as a reward for all her misdemeanors. Her vileness and God's holiness and all-pervading presence, which filled immensity, and threatened her with instant annihilation, composed the burden of her vision of terror. Her faith in prayer is equal to her faith in the love of Jesus. Her language is, "Let others say what they will of the efficacy of prayer, *I* believe in it, and *I* shall pray. Thank God! Yes, *I shall always pray,*" she exclaims, putting her hands together with the greatest enthusiasm.

For sometime subsequent to the happy change we have spoken of, Isabella's prayers partook largely of their former character; and while, in deep affliction, she labored for the recovery of her son, she prayed with constancy and fervor; and the following may be taken as a specimen:—"Oh, God, you know how much I am distressed, for I have told you again and again. Now, God, help me get my son. If you were in trouble, as I am, and I could help you, as you can me, think I would n't do it? Yes, God, you *know* I would do it." "Oh, God, you know I have no money, but you can make the people do for me, and you must make the people do for me. I will never give you peace till you do, God." "Oh, God, make the people hear me—don't let them turn me off, without hearing and helping me." And she has not a particle of doubt, that God heard her, and especially disposed the hearts of thoughtless clerks, eminent lawyers, and grave judges and others—between whom and herself there seemed to her almost an infinite remove—to listen to her suit with patient and respectful attention, backing it up with all needed aid. The sense of her nothingness, in the eyes of those with whom she contended for her rights, sometimes fell on her like a heavy weight, which nothing but her unwavering confidence in an arm which she believed to be stronger than all others combined could have raised from her sinking spirit. "Oh! how little I did feel," she repeated, with a powerful emphasis. "Neither would you wonder, if you could have seen me, in my ignorance and destitution, trotting about the streets, meanly clad, bare-headed, and bare-footed! Oh, God only could have made such people hear me; and he did it in answer to my prayers." And this perfect trust, based on the rock of Deity, was a soul-protecting fortress, which, raising her above the battlements of fear, and shielding her from the machinations of the enemy, impelled her onward in the struggle, till the foe was vanquished, and the victory gained.

We have now seen Isabella, her youngest daughter, and her only son, in possession of, at least, their nominal freedom. It has been said that the freedom of the most free of the colored people of this country is but nominal; but stinted and limited as it is, at best, it is an *immense* remove from chattel slavery. This fact is disputed, I know; but I have no confidence in the honesty of such questionings. If they are made in sincerity, I honor not the judgment that thus decides.

Her husband, quite advanced in age, and infirm of health, was emancipated, with the balance of the adult slaves of the State, according to law, the following summer, July 4, 1828.[16]

For a few years after this event, he was able to earn a scanty living, and when he failed to do that, he was dependant on the "world's cold charity," and died in a poor-house. Isabella had herself and two children to provide for; her wages were trifling, for at that time the wages of females were at a small advance from nothing; and she doubtless had to learn the first elements of economy—for what slaves, that were never allowed to make any stipulations or calculations for themselves, ever possessed an adequate idea of the true value of time, or, in fact, of any material thing in the universe? To such, "prudent using" is meanness—and "saving" is a word to be sneered at. Of course, it was not in her power to make to herself a home, around whose sacred hearth-stone she could collect her family, as they gradually emerged from their prison-house of bondage; a home, where she could cultivate their affection, administer to their wants, and instil into the opening minds of her children those principles of virtue, and that love of purity, truth, and benevolence, which must ever form the foundation of a life of usefulness and happiness. No—all this was far beyond her power or means, in more senses than one; and it should be taken into the account, whenever a comparison is instituted between the progress made by her children in virtue and goodness, and the progress of those who have been nurtured in the genial warmth of a sunny home, where good influences cluster, and bad ones are carefully excluded—where "line upon line, and precept upon precept," are daily brought to their quotidian tasks—and where, in short, every appliance is brought in requisition, that self-denying parents *can* bring to bear on one of the dearest objects of a parent's life, the promotion of the welfare of their children. But God forbid that this suggestion should be wrested from its original intent, and made to shield any one from merited rebuke! Isabella's children are now of an age to know good from evil, and may easily inform themselves on any point where they may yet be in doubt; and if they now suffer themselves to be drawn by temptation into the paths of the destroyer, or forget what is due to the mother who has done and suffered so much for them, and who, now that she is descending into the vale of years and feels her health and strength declining, will turn her expecting eyes to them for aid and comfort, just as instinctly as the child turns its confiding eye to its fond parent, when it seeks for succor or for sympathy—(for it is now their turn to do the work, and bear the burdens of life, as all must bear them in turn, as the wheel of life rolls on)—if, I say, they forget this, their duty and their happiness, and pursue an opposite course of sin and folly, they must lose the respect of the wise and good, and find, when too late, that "the way of the transgressor is hard."

NEW TRIALS

The reader will pardon this passing homily, while we return to our narrative.

We were saying that the day-dreams of Isabella and her

husband—the plan they drew of what they would do, and the comforts they thought to have, when they should obtain their freedom, and a little home of their own—had all turned to "thin air," by the postponement of their freedom to so late a day. These delusive hopes were never to be realized, and a new set of trials was gradually to open before her. These were the heart-wasting trials of watching over her children, scattered, and imminently exposed to the temptations of the adversary, with few, if any, fixed principles to sustain them.

"Oh," she says, "how little did I know myself of the best way to instruct and counsel them! Yet I did the best I then knew, when with them. I took them to the religious meetings; I talked to, and prayed for and with them; when they did wrong, I scolded at and whipped them."

Isabella and her son had been free about a year, when they went to reside in the city of New York; a place which she would doubtless have avoided, could she have seen what was there in store for her; for this view into the future would have taught her what she only learned by bitter experience, that the baneful influences going up from such a city were not the best helps to education, commenced as the education of *her* children had been.

Her son Peter was, at the time of which we are speaking, just at that age when no lad should be subjected to the temptations of such a place, unprotected as he was, save by the feeble arm of a mother, herself a servant there. He was growing up to be a tall, well-formed, active lad, of quick perceptions, mild and cheerful in his disposition, with much that was open, generous, and winning about him, but with little power to withstand temptation, and a ready ingenuity to provide himself with ways and means to carry out his plans, and conceal from his mother and her friends, all such as he knew would not meet their approbation. As will be readily believed, he was soon drawn into a circle of associates who did not improve either his habits or his morals.

Two years passed before Isabella knew what character Peter was establishing for himself among his low and worthless comrades—passing under the assumed name of Peter Williams; and she began to feel a parent's pride in the promising appearance of her only son. But, alas! this pride and pleasure were shortly dissipated, as distressing facts relative to him came one by one to her astonished ear. A friend of Isabella's, a lady, who was much pleased with the good humor, ingenuity, and open confessions of Peter, when driven into a corner, and who, she said, "was so smart, he ought to have an education, if any one ought"—paid ten dollars, as tuition fee, for him to attend a navigation school. But Peter, little inclined to spend his leisure hours in study, when he might be enjoying himself in the dance, or otherwise, with his boon companions, went regularly and made some plausible excuses to the teacher, who received them as genuine, along with the ten dollars of Mrs.———, and while his mother and her friend believed him improving at school, he was, to their latent sorrow, improving in a very different place or places, and on entirely opposite principles. They also procured him an excellent place as a coachman. But, wanting money, he sold his livery, and other things belonging to his master; who, having conceived a kind regard for him, considered his youth, and prevented the law from falling, with all its rigor, upon his head. Still he continued to abuse his privileges, and to involve himself in repeated difficulties, from which his mother as often extricated him. At each time, she talked much, and reasoned and remonstrated with him; and he would, with such perfect frankness, lay open his whole soul to her, telling her he had never intended doing harm,—how he had been led along, little by little, till, before he was aware, he found himself in trouble—how he had *tried* to be good—and how, when he would have been so, "evil was present with him,"—indeed he knew not *how* it was.

His mother, beginning to feel that the city was no place for

him, urged his going to sea, and would have shipped him on
board a man-of-war; but Peter was not disposed to consent to
that proposition, while the city and its pleasures were accessible
to him. Isabella now became a prey to distressing fears, dreading
lest the next day or hour come fraught with the report of some
dreadful crime, committed or abetted by her son. She thanks the
Lord for sparing her that giant sorrow, as all his wrong doings
never ranked higher, in the eye of the law, than misdemeanors.
But as she could see no improvement in Peter, as a last resort,
she resolved to leave him, for a time, unassisted, to bear the
penalty of his conduct, and see what effect that would have on
him. In the trial hour, she remained firm in her resolution. Peter
again fell into the hands of the police, and sent for his mother,
as usual; but she went not to his relief. In his extremity, he sent
for Peter Williams, a respectable colored barber, whose name he
had been wearing, and who sometimes helped young culprits
out of their troubles, and sent them from city dangers, by ship-
ping them on board of whaling vessels.

The curiosity of this man was awakened by the culprit's
bearing his own name. He went to the Tombs and inquired
into his case, but could not believe what Peter told him respecting his mother and family. Yet he redeemed him, and
Peter promised to leave New York in a vessel that was to sail
in the course of a week. He went to see his mother, and informed her of what had happened to him. She listened in-
credulously, as to an idle tale. He asked her to go with him
and see for herself. She went, giving no credence to his story
till she found herself in the presence of Mr. Williams, and
heard him saying to her, "I am very glad I have assisted your
son; he stood in great need of sympathy and assistance; but I
could not think he had such a mother here, although he assured me he had."

Isabella's great trouble now was, a fear lest her son should
deceive his benefactor, and be missing when the vessel sailed;

but he begged her earnestly to trust him, for he said he had resolved to do better, and meant to abide by the resolve. Isabella's heart gave her no peace till the time of sailing, when Peter sent Mr. Williams and another messenger whom she knew, to tell her he had sailed. But for a month afterwards, she looked to see him emerging from some by-place in the city, and appearing before her; so afraid was she that he was still unfaithful, and doing wrong. But he did not appear, and at length she believed him really gone. He left in the summer of 1839, and his friends heard nothing further from him till his mother received the following letter, dated "October 17, 1840":—

"My Dear and Beloved Mother:

"I take this opportunity to write to you and inform you that I am well, and in hopes for to find you the same. I am got on board the same unlucky ship Done,[17] of Nantucket. I am sorry for to say, that I have been punished once severely, by shoving my head in the fire for other folks. We have had bad luck, but in hopes to have better. We have about 230 on board, but in hopes, if do n't have good luck, that my parents will receive me with thanks. I would like to know how my sisters are. Does my cousins live in New York yet? Have you got my letter? If not, inquire to Mr. Peirce Whiting's. I wish you would write me an answer as soon as possible. I am your only son, that is so far from your home, in the wide, briny ocean. I have seen more of the world than ever I expected, and if I ever should return home safe, I will tell you all my troubles and hardships. Mother, I hope you do not forget me, your dear and only son. I should like to know how Sophia, and Betsey, and Hannah,[18] come on. I hope you all will forgive me for all that I have done.

"Your son,
"PETER VAN WAGENER."

Another letter reads as follows, dated "March 22, 1841":

"My Dear Mother:

"I take this opportunity to write to you, and inform
you that I have been well and in good health. I have wrote
you a letter before, but have received no answer from you,
and was very anxious to see you. I hope to see you in a
short time. I have had very hard luck, but are in hopes to
have better in time to come. I should like if my sisters are
well, and all the people round the neighborhood. I expect
to be home in twenty-two months or thereabouts. I have
seen Samuel Laterett. Beware! There has happened very
bad news to tell you, that Peter Jackson is dead. He died
within two days' sail of Otaheite, one of the Society Is-
lands. The Peter Jackson that used to live at Laterett's;
he died on board the ship Done, of Nantucket, Captain
Miller, in the latitude 15 53, and longitude 148 30 W. I
have no more to say at present, but write as soon as
possible.

"Your only son,
"PETER VAN WAGENER."

Another, containing the last intelligence she has had from her
son, reads as follows, and was dated "Sept. 19, 1841":

"Dear Mother:

"I take this opportunity to write to you and inform you
that I am well and in good health, and in hopes to find you
in the same. This is the fifth letter I have wrote you, and
have received no answer, and it makes me very uneasy.
So pray write as quick as you can, and tell how all the
people is about the neighborhood. We are out from home
twenty-three months, and in hopes to be home in fifteen
months. I have not much to say; but tell me if you have

been up home since I left or not. I want to know what sort
of a time is at home. We had very bad luck when we first
came out, but since we have had very good; so I am in
hopes to do well yet; but if I do n't do well, you need not
expect me home these five years. So write as quick as you
can, wont you? So, now I am going to put an end to my
writing, at present. Notice—when this you see, remember
me, and place me in your mind.

Get me to my home, that's in the far-distant west,
To the scenes of my childhood, that I like the best;
There the tall cedars grow, and the bright waters flow,
Where my parents will greet me, white man, let me go!

Let me go to the spot where the cateract plays,
Where oft I have sported in my boyish days;
And there is my poor mother, whose heart ever flows,
At the sight of her poor child, to her let me go,
  let me go!

> "Your only son,
> "PETER VAN WAGENER."

Since the date of the last letter, Isabella has heard no tidings
from her long-absent son, though ardently does her mother's
heart long for such tidings, as her thoughts follow him around
the world, in his perilous vocation, saying within herself—"He
is good now, I have no doubt; I feel sure that he has persevered,
and kept the resolve he made before he left home;—he seemed
so different before he went, so determined to do better." His
letters are inserted here for preservation, in case they prove the
last she ever hears from him in this world.

FINDING A BROTHER AND SISTER

When Isabella had obtained the freedom of her son, she remained in Kingston, where she had been drawn by the judicial
process, about a year, during which time she became a member
of the Methodist Church there; and when she went to New
York, she took a letter missive from that church to the Methodist Church in John street. Afterwards, she withdrew her connection with that church, and joined Zion's Church, in Church
street, composed entirely of colored people. With the latter
church she remained until she went to reside with Mr. Pierson,
after which, she was gradually drawn into the "kingdom" set up
by the prophet Matthias, in the name of God the Father; for he
said the spirit of God the Father dwelt in him.

While Isabella was in New York, her sister Sophia came from
Newberg to reside in the former place. Isabel had been favored
with occasional interviews with this sister, although at one time
she lost sight of her for the space of seventeen years—almost the
entire period of her being at Mr. Dumont's—and when she
appeared before her again, handsomely dressed, she did not
recognize her, till informed who she was. Sophia informed her
that her brother Michael—a brother she had never seen—was in
the city; and when she introduced him to Isabella, *he* informed
her that their sister Nancy had been living in the city, and had
deceased a few months before. He described her features, her
dress, her manner, and said she had for some time been a member in Zion's Church, naming the class she belonged to. Isabella
almost instantly recognized her as a sister in the church, with
whom she had knelt at the altar, and with whom she had exchanged the speaking pressure of the hand, in recognition of
their spiritual sisterhood; little thinking, at the time, that they
were also children of the same earthly parents—even Bomefree

and Mau-mau Bett. As inquiries and answers rapidly passed, and
the conviction deepened that this was their sister, the very sister
they had heard so much of, but had never seen, (for she was the
self-same sister that had been locked in the great old-fashioned
sleigh-box, when she was taken away, never to behold her
mother's face again this side of the spirit-land, and Michael, the
narrator, was the brother who had shared her fate,) Isabella
thought, "D——h![19] here she was; we met; and was I not, at the
time, struck with the peculiar feeling of her hand—the bony
hardness so just like mine? and yet I could not know she was my
sister; and now I see she looked *so* like my mother!" And Isabella
wept, and not alone; Sophia wept, and the strong man, Michael,
mingled his tears with theirs. "Oh Lord," inquired Isabella,
"what is this slavery, that it can do such dreadful things? what
evil can it not do?" Well may she ask; for surely the evils it can
and does do, daily and hourly, can never be summed up, till we
can see them as they are recorded by him who writes no errors,
and reckons without mistake. This account, which now varies
so widely in the estimate of different minds, will be viewed alike
by all.

Think you, dear reader, when that day comes, the most
"rabid abolitionist" will say—"Behold, I saw all this while on
the earth"? Will he not rather say, "Oh, who has conceived the
breadth and depth of this moral malaria, this putrescent plague-
spot"? Perhaps the pioneers in the slave's cause will be as much
surprised as any to find that with all *their* looking, there remained
so much unseen.

GLEANINGS

There are some hard things that crossed Isabella's life while in
slavery, that she has no desire to publish, for various reasons.

First, because the parties from whose hands she suffered them have rendered up their account to a higher tribunal, and their innocent friends alone are living, to have their feelings injured by the recital; secondly, because they are not all for the public ear, from their very nature; thirdly, and not least, because, she says, were she to tell all that happened to her as a slave—all that she knows is "God's truth"—it would seem to others, especially the uninitiated, so unaccountable, so unreasonable, and what is usually called so unnatural, (though it may be questioned whether people do not always act naturally,) they would not easily believe it. "Why, no!" she says, "they'd call me a liar! they would, indeed! and I do not wish to say any thing to destroy my own character for veracity, though what I say is strictly true." Some things have been omitted through forgetfulness, which not having been mentioned in their places, can only be briefly spoken of here;—such as, that her father Bomefree had had two wives before he took Mau-mau Bett; one of whom, if not both, were torn from him by the iron hand of the ruthless trafficker in human flesh;—that her husband, Thomas, after one of *his* wives had been sold away from him, ran away to New York city, where he remained a year or two, before he was discovered and taken back to the prison-house of slavery;—that her master Dumont, when he promised Isabella one year of her time, before the State should make her free, made the same promise to her husband, and in addition to freedom, they were promised a log cabin for a home of their own; all of which, with the one-thousand-and-one day-dreams resulting therefrom, went into the repository of unfulfilled promises and unrealized hopes;— that she had often heard her father repeat a thrilling story of a little slave-child, which, because it annoyed the family with its cries, was caught up by a white man, who dashed its brains out against the wall. An Indian (for Indians were plenty in that region then) passed along as the bereaved mother washed the bloody corpse of her murdered child, and learning the cause of

its death, said, with characteristic vehemence, "If I had been here, I would have put my tomahawk in his head!" meaning the murderer's.

Of the cruelty of one Hasbrouck.—He had a sick slave-woman, who was lingering with a slow consumption, whom he made to spin, regardless of her weakness and suffering; and this woman had a child, that was unable to walk or talk, at the age of five years, neither could it cry like other children, but made a constant, piteous, moaning sound. This exhibition of helplessness and imbecility, instead of exciting the master's pity, stung his cupidity, and so enraged him, that he would kick the poor thing about like a foot-ball.

Isabella's informant had seen this brute of a man, when the child was curled up under a chair, innocently amusing itself with a few sticks, drag it thence, that he might have the pleasure of tormenting it. She had seen him, with one blow of his foot, send it rolling quite across the room and down the steps at the door. Oh, how she wished it might instantly die! "But," she said, "it seemed as tough as a moccasin." Though it *did* die at last, and made glad the heart of its friends; and its persecutor, no doubt, rejoiced with them, but from very different motives. But the day of his retribution was not far off—for he sickened, and his reason fled. It was fearful to hear his old slave soon tell how, in the day of his calamity, she treated *him*.

She was very strong, and was therefore selected to support her master, as he sat up in bed, by putting her arms around, while she stood behind him. It was then that she did her best to wreak her vengeance on him. She would clutch his feeble frame in her iron grasp, as in a vice; and, when her mistress did not see, would give him a squeeze, a shake, and lifting him up, set him down again, as *hard as possible*. If his breathing betrayed too tight a grasp, and her mistress said, "Be careful, don't hurt him, Soan!" her ever-ready answer was, "Oh, no, Missus, no" in her most pleasant tone—and then, as soon as Missus's eyes and ears were engaged away, another grasp—another shake—another bounce. She was afraid the disease alone would let him recover,—an event she dreaded more than to do wrong herself. Isabella asked her, if she were not afraid his spirit would haunt her. "Oh, no," says Soan; "he was *so* wicked, the devil will never let him out of hell long enough for that."

Many slaveholders boast of the love of their slaves. How would it freeze the blood of some of them to know what kind of love rankles in the bosoms of slaves for them! Witness the attempt to poison Mrs. Calhoun, and hundreds of similar cases. Most *"surprising"* to every body, because committed by slaves supposed to be so *grateful* for their chains.

These reflections bring to mind a discussion on this point, between the writer and a slaveholding friend in Kentucky, on Christmas morning, 1846. We had asserted, that until mankind were far in advance of what they now are, irresponsible power over our fellow-beings would be, as it is, abused. Our friend declared it *his* conviction, that the cruelties of slavery existed chiefly in imagination, and that no person in D—— County, where we then were, but would be above ill-treating a helpless slave. We answered, that if his belief was well-founded, the people in Kentucky were greatly in advance of the people of New England—for we would not dare say as much as that of any school-district there, letting alone counties. No, we would not answer for our own conduct even on so delicate a point.

The next evening, he very magnanimously overthrew his own position and established ours, by informing us that, on the morning previous, and as near as we could learn, at the very hour in which we were earnestly discussing the probabilities of the case, a young woman of fine appearance, and high standing in society, the pride of her husband, and the mother of an infant daughter, only a few miles from us, ay, in D—— County, too, was actually beating in the skull of a slave-woman called Tabby; and not content with that, had her tied up and whipped, after her skull was broken, and she died hanging to the bedstead, to which she had been fastened. When informed that Tabby was dead, she answered, "I am *glad of it,* for she has worried my life out of me." But Tabby's highest good was probably not the end proposed by Mrs. M——, for no one supposed she meant to kill her. Tabby was considered quite lacking in good sense, and no doubt belonged to that class at the South, that are silly enough to "die of moderate correction."

A mob collected around the house for an hour or two in that manner expressing a momentary indignation. But was she treated as a murderess? Not at all! She was allowed to take boat (for her residence was near the beautiful Ohio) that evening, to spend a few months with her absent friends, after which she returned and remained with her husband, no one to "molest or make her afraid."

Had she been left to the punishment of an outraged conscience from right motives, I would have "rejoiced with exceeding joy." But to see the life of one woman, and she a murderess, put in the balance against the lives of three millions of innocent slaves, and to contrast her punishment with what I felt would be the punishment of one who was merely suspected of being an equal friend of all mankind, regardless of color or condition, caused my blood to stir within me, and my heart to sicken at the thought. The husband of Mrs. M—— was absent from home, at the time alluded to; and when he arrived some weeks afterwards, bringing beautiful presents to his cherished companion, he beheld his once happy home deserted, Tabby murdered and buried in the garden, and the wife of his bosom, and the mother of his child, the doer of the dreadful deed, a *murderess!*

When Isabella went to New York city, she went in company with a Miss Gear, who introduced her to the family of Mr. James Latourette, a wealthy merchant, and a Methodist in religion; but who, the latter part of his life, felt that he had outgrown ordinances, and advocated free meetings, holding them at his own dwelling-house for several years previous to his death. She worked for them, and they generously gave her a home while she labored for others, and in their kindness made her as one of their own.

At that time, the "moral reform" movement was awakening the attention of the benevolent in that city. Many women, among whom were Mrs. Latourette and Miss Gear, became deeply interested in making an attempt to reform their fallen sisters, even the most degraded of them; and in this enterprise of labor and danger, they enlisted Isabella and others, who for a time put forth their most zealous efforts, and performed the work of missionaries with much apparent success. Isabella accompanied those ladies to the most wretched abodes of vice and misery, and sometimes she went where they dared not follow. They even succeeded in establishing prayer-meetings in several places, where such a thing might least have been expected.

But these meetings soon became the most noisy, shouting, ranting, and boisterous of gatherings; where they became delirious with excitement, and then exhausted from over-action. Such meetings Isabel had not much sympathy with, at best. But one evening she attended one of them, where the members of it, in a fit of ecstasy, jumped upon her cloak in such a manner as to drag her to the floor—and then, thinking she had fallen in a spiritual trance, they increased their glorifications on her account,—jumping, shouting, stamping, and clapping of hands; rejoicing so much over her spirit, and so entirely overlooking her body, that she suffered much, both from fear and bruises; and ever after refused to attend any more such meetings, doubting much whether God had any thing to do with such worship.

THE MATTHIAS IMPOSTURE

We now come to an eventful period in the life of Isabella, as identified with one of the most extraordinary religious impostures of modern times; but the limits prescribed for the present work forbid a minute narration of all the occurrences that transpired in relation to it.

After she had joined the African Church in Church street, and during her membership there, she frequently attended Mr. Latourette's meetings, at one of which Mr. Smith invited her to go to a prayer-meeting, or to instruct the girls at the Magdalene Asylum, Bowery Hill, then under the protection of Mr. Pierson, and some other persons, chiefly respectable females. To reach the Asylum, Isabella called on Katy, Mr. Pierson's colored servant, of whom she had some knowledge. Mr. Pierson saw her there, conversed with her, asked her if she had been baptized, and was answered, characteristically, "by the Holy Ghost." After this, Isabella saw Katy several times, and occasionally Mr. Pierson, who engaged her to keep his house while Katy went to Virginia to see her children. This engagement was considered an answer to prayer by Mr. Pierson, who had both fasted and prayed on the subject, while Katy and Isabella appeared to see in it the hand of God.

Mr. Pierson was characterised by a strong devotional spirit, which finally became highly fanatical. He assumed the title of Prophet, asserting that God had called him in an omnibus, in these words:—"Thou art Elijah, the Tishbite. Gather unto me all the members of Israel at the foot of Mount Carmel"; which he understood as meaning the gathering of his friends at Bowery Hill. Not long afterward, he became acquainted with the notorious Matthias, whose career was as extraordinary as it was brief. Robert Matthews, or Matthias, (as he was usually called,) was of

Scotch extraction, but a native of Washington county, New
York, and at that time about forty-seven years of age. He was
religiously brought up, among the Anti-Burghers, a sect of Pres-
byterians; the clergyman, the Rev. Mr. Bevridge, visiting the
family after the manner of the church, and being pleased with
Robert, put his hand on his head, when a boy, and pronounced
a blessing, and this blessing, with his natural qualities, determined his character; for he ever after thought he should be a
distinguished man. Matthias was brought up a farmer till nearly
eighteen years of age, but acquired indirectly the art of a carpen-
ter, without any regular apprenticeship, and showed considerable mechanical skill. He obtained property from his uncle,
Robert Thompson, and then he went into business as a store-
keeper, was considered respectable, and became a member of the
Scotch Presbyterian Church. He married in 1813, and continued in business in Cambridge. In 1816, he ruined himself by
a building speculation, and the derangement of the currency
which denied bank facilities, and soon after he came to New
York with his family and worked at his trade. He afterwards
removed to Albany, and became a hearer at the Dutch Reformed Church, then under Dr. Ludlow's charge. He was frequently much excited on religious subjects.

In 1829, he was well known, if not for street preaching, for
loud discussions and pavement exhortations, but he did not
make set sermons. In the beginning of 1830, he was only considered zealous; but in the same year he prophesied the destruction
of the Albanians and their capital, and while preparing to shave,
with the Bible before him, he suddenly put down the soap and
exclaimed, "I have found it! I have found a text which proves
that no man who shaves his beard can be a true Christian"; and
shortly afterwards, without shaving, he went to the Mission
House to deliver an address which he had promised, and in this
address he proclaimed his new character, pronounced vengeance
on the land, and that the law of God was the only rule of

government, and that he was commanded to take possession of the world in the name of the King of kings. His harangue was cut short by the trustees putting out the lights. About this time, Matthias laid by his implements of industry, and in June, he advised his wife to fly with him from the destruction which awaited them in the city; and on her refusal, partly on account of Matthias calling himself a Jew, whom she was unwilling to retain as a husband, he left her, taking some of the children to his sister in Argyle, forty miles from Albany. At Argyle he entered the church and interrupted the minister, declaring the congregation in darkness, and warning them to repentance. He was, of course, taken out of the church, and as he was advertised in the Albany papers, he was sent back to his family. His beard had now obtained a respectable length, and thus he attracted attention, and easily obtained an audience in the streets. For this he was sometimes arrested, once by mistake for Adam Paine, who collected the crowd, and then left Matthias with it on the approach of the officers. He repeatedly urged his wife to accompany him on a mission to convert the world, declaring that food could be obtained from the roots of the forest, if not administered otherwise. At this time he assumed the name of Matthias, called himself a Jew, and set out on a mission, taking a western course, and visiting a brother at Rochester, a skillful mechanic, since dead. Leaving his brother, he proceeded on his mission over the Northern States, occasionally returning to Albany.

After visiting Washington, and passing through Pennsylvania, he came to New York. His appearance at that time was mean, but grotesque, and his sentiments were but little known.

On May the 5th, 1832, he first called on Mr. Pierson, in Fourth street, in his absence. Isabella was alone in the house, in which she had lived since the previous autumn. On opening the door, she, for the first time, beheld Matthias, and her early impression of seeing Jesus in the flesh rushed into her mind. She heard his inquiry, and invited him into the parlor; and being naturally curious, and much excited, and possessing a good deal of tact, she drew him into conversation, stated her own opinions, and heard his replies and explanations. Her faith was at first staggered by his declaring himself a Jew; but on this point she was relieved by his saying, "Do you not remember how Jesus prayed?" and repeated part of the Lord's prayer, in proof that the Father's kingdom was to come, and not the Son's. She then understood him to be a converted Jew, and in the conclusion she says she "*felt* as if God had sent him to set up the kingdom." Thus Matthias at once secured the good will of Isabella, and we may suppose obtained from her some information in relation to Mr. Pierson, especially that Mrs. Pierson declared there was no true church, and approved of Mr. Pierson's preaching. Matthias left the house, promising to return on Saturday evening. Mr. P. at this time had not seen Matthias.

Isabella, desirous of hearing the expected conversation between Matthias and Mr. Pierson on Saturday, hurried her work, got it finished, and was permitted to be present. Indeed, the sameness of belief made her familiar with her employer, while her attention to her work, and characteristic faithfulness, increased his confidence. This intimacy, the result of holding the same faith, and the principle afterwards adopted of having but one table, and all things in common, made her at once the domestic and the equal, and the depository of very curious, if not valuable information. To this object, even her color assisted. Persons who have travelled in the South know the manner in which the colored people, and especially slaves, are treated; they are scarcely regarded as being present. This trait in our American character has been frequently noticed by foreign travellers. One English lady remarks that she discovered, in course of conversation with a Southern married gentleman, that a colored girl slept in his bedroom, in which also was his wife; and when he saw that it occasioned some surprise, he remarked, "What would he do if he wanted a glass of water in the night?" Other travellers have remarked that the presence of colored people never seemed to interrupt conversation of any kind for one moment. Isabella, then, was present at the first interview between Matthias and Pierson. At this interview, Mr. Pierson asked Matthias if he had a family, to which he replied in the affirmative; he asked him about his beard, and he gave a scriptural reason, asserting also that the Jews did not shave, and that Adam had a beard. Mr. Pierson detailed to Matthias his experience, and Matthias gave his, and they mutually discovered that they held the same sentiments, both admitting the direct influence of the Spirit, and the transmission of spirits from one body to another. Matthias admitted the call of Mr. Pierson, in the omnibus in Wall street, which, on this occasion, he gave in these words:—"Thou art Elijah the Tishbite, and thou shalt go before me in the spirit and power of Elias, to prepare my way before me." And Mr. Pierson admitted Matthias' call, who *completed* his declaration on the 20th of June, in Argyle, which, by a curious coincidence, was the very day on which Pierson had received his call in the omnibus. Such singular coincidences have a powerful effect on excited minds. From that discovery, Pierson and Matthias rejoiced in each other, and became kindred spirits—Matthias, however, claiming to be the Father, or to possess the spirit of the Father—he was God upon earth, because the spirit of God dwelt in him; while Pierson then understood that his mission was like that of John the Baptist, which the name Elias meant. This conference ended with an invitation to supper, and Matthias and Pierson washing each other's feet. Mr. Pierson preached on the following Sunday, but after which, he declined in favor of Matthias, and some of the party believed that the "kingdom had then come."

As a specimen of Matthias' preaching and sentiments, the following is said to be reliable:—

"The spirit that built the Tower of Babel is now in the world—it is the spirit of the devil. The spirit of man never goes upon the clouds; all who think so are Babylonians. The only heaven is on the earth. All who are ignorant of truth are Ninevites. The Jews did not crucify Christ—it was the Gentiles. Every Jew has his guardian angel attending him in this world. God don't speak through preachers; he speaks through me, his prophet.

" 'John the Baptist,' (addressing Mr. Pierson,) read the tenth chapter of Revelations." After the reading of the chapter, the prophet resumed speaking, as follows:—

"Ours is the mustard-seed kingdom which is to spread all over the earth. Our creed is truth, and no man can find truth unless he obeys John the Baptist, and comes clean into the church.

"All *real* men will be saved; all *mock* men will be damned. When a person has the Holy Ghost, then he is a man, and not till then. They who teach women are of the wicked. The communion is all nonsense; so is prayer. Eating a nip of bread and drinking a little wine won't do any good. All who admit members into their church, and suffer them to hold their lands and houses, their sentence is, 'Depart, ye wicked, I know you not.' All females who lecture their husbands, their sentence is the same. The sons of truth are to enjoy all the good things of this world, and must use their means to bring it about. Every thing that has the smell of woman will be destroyed. Woman is the capsheaf of the abomination of desolation—full of all deviltry. In a short time, the world will take fire and dissolve; it is combustible already. All women, not obedient, had better become so as soon as possible, and let the wicked spirit depart, and become temples of truth. Praying is all mocking. When you see any one wring the neck of a fowl, instead of cutting off its head, he has not got the Holy Ghost. (Cutting gives the least pain.)

"All who eat swine's flesh are of the devil; and just as certain as he eats it, he will tell a lie in less than half an hour. If you eat a piece of pork, it will go crooked through you, and the Holy

Ghost will not stay in you, but one or the other must leave the house pretty soon. The pork will be as crooked in you as ram's horns, and as great a nuisance as the hogs in the street.

"The cholera is not the right word; it is choler, which means God's wrath. Abraham, Isaac, and Jacob are now in this world; they did not go up in the clouds, as some believe—why should they go there? They don't want to go there to box the compass from one place to another. The Christians now-a-days are for setting up the *Son's* kingdom. It is not his; it is the *Father's* kingdom. It puts me in mind of the man in the country, who took his son in business, and had his sign made, 'Hitchcock & Son'; but the son wanted it 'Hitchcock & Father'—and that is the way with your Christians. They talk of the Son's kingdom first, and not the Father's kingdom."

Matthias and his disciples at this time did not believe in a resurrection of the body, but that the spirits of the former saints would enter the bodies of the present generation, and thus begin heaven upon earth, of which he and Mr. Pierson were the first fruits.

Matthias made the residence of Mr. Pierson his own; but the latter, being apprehensive of popular violence in his house, if Matthias remained there, proposed a monthly allowance to him, and advised him to occupy another dwelling. Matthias accordingly took a house in Clarkson street, and then sent for his family at Albany, but they declined coming to the city. However, his brother George complied with a similar offer, bringing his family with him, where they found very comfortable quarters. Isabella was employed to do the housework. In May, 1833, Matthias left his house, and placed the furniture, part of which was Isabella's, elsewhere, living himself at the hotel corner of Marketfield and West streets. Isabella found employment at Mr. Whiting's, Canal street, and did the washing for Matthias, by Mrs. Whiting's permission.

Of the subsequent removal of Matthias to the farm and residence of Mr. B. Folger, at Sing Sing, where he was joined by Mr. Pierson, and others laboring under a similar religious delusion—the sudden, melancholy, and somewhat suspicious death of Mr. Pierson, and the arrest of Matthias on the charge of his murder, ending in a verdict of not guilty—the criminal connection that subsisted between Matthias, Mrs. Folger, and other members of the "kingdom," as "match-spirits"—the final dispersion of this deluded company, and the voluntary exilement of Matthias in the far West, after his release—&c. &c., we do not deem it useful or necessary to give any particulars. Those who are curious to know what there transpired are referred to a work published in New York in 1835, entitled "Fanaticism; its Sources and Influence; illustrated by the simple Narrative of Isabella, in the case of Matthias, Mr. and Mrs. B. Folger, Mr. Pierson, Mr. Mills, Catharine, Isabella, &c. &c. By G. Vale, 84 Roosevelt street." Suffice it to say, that while Isabella was a member of the household at Sing Sing, doing much laborious service in the spirit of religious disinterestedness, and gradually getting her vision purged and her mind cured of its illusions, she happily escaped the contamination that surrounded her, assiduously endeavoring to discharge all her duties in a becoming manner.

FASTING

When Isabella resided with Mr. Pierson, he was in the habit of fasting every Friday; not eating or drinking any thing from Thursday evening to six o'clock on Friday evening.

Then, again, he would fast two nights and three days, neither eating nor drinking; refusing himself even a cup of cold water till the third day at night, when he took supper again, as usual.

Isabella asked him why he fasted. He answered, that fasting

gave him great light in the things of God; which answer gave birth to the following train of thought in the mind of his auditor: —"Well, if fasting will give light inwardly and spiritually, I need it as much as any body,—and I'll fast too. If Mr. Pierson needs to fast two nights and three days, then I, who need light more than he does, ought to fast more, and I will fast three nights and three days."

This resolution she carried out to the letter, putting not so much as a drop of water in her mouth for three whole days and nights. The fourth morning, as she arose to her feet, not having power to stand, she fell to the floor; but recovering herself sufficiently, she made her way to the pantry, and feeling herself quite voracious, and fearing that she might now offend God by her voracity, compelled herself to breakfast on dry bread and water—eating a large six-penny loaf before she felt at all stayed or satisfied. She says she did get light, but it was all in her body and none in her mind—and this lightness of body lasted a long time. Oh! she was so light, and felt so well, she could "skim around like a gull."

THE CAUSE OF HER LEAVING THE CITY

The first years spent by Isabella in the city, she accumulated more than enough to supply all her wants, and she placed all the overplus in the Savings' Bank. Afterwards, while living with Mr. Pierson, he prevailed on her to take it thence, and invest it in a common fund which he was about establishing, as a fund to be drawn from by all the faithful; the faithful, of course, were the handful that should subscribe to his peculiar creed. This fund, commenced by Mr. Pierson, afterwards became part and parcel of the kingdom of which Matthias assumed to be head; and at the breaking up of the kingdom, her little property was merged in the general ruin—or went to enrich those who profited by the loss of others, if any such there were. Mr. Pierson and others had so assured her, that the fund would supply all her wants, at all times, and in all emergencies, and to the end of life, that she became perfectly careless on the subject—asking for no interest when she drew her money from the bank, and taking no account of the sum she placed in the fund. She recovered a few articles of furniture from the wreck of the kingdom, and received a small sum of money from Mr. B. Folger, as the price of Mrs. Folger's attempt to convict her of murder. With this to start upon, she commenced anew her labors, in the hope of yet being able to accumulate a sufficiency to make a little home for herself, in her advancing age. With this stimulus before her, she toiled hard, working early and late, doing a great deal for a little money, and turning her hand to almost any thing that promised good pay. Still, she did not prosper; and somehow, could not contrive to lay by a single dollar for a "rainy day."

When this had been the state of her affairs some time, she suddenly paused, and taking a retrospective view of what had passed, inquired within herself, why it was that, for all her unwearied labors, she had nothing to show; why it was that others, with much less care and labor, could hoard up treasures for themselves and children? She became more and more convinced, as she reasoned, that every thing she had undertaken in the city of New York had finally proved a failure; and where her hopes had been raised the highest, there she felt the failure had been the greatest, and the disappointment most severe.

After turning it in her mind for some time, she came to the conclusion, that she had been taking part in a great drama, which was, in itself, but one great system of robbery and wrong. "Yes," she said, "the rich rob the poor, and the poor rob one another." True, she had not received labor from others, and stinted their pay, as she felt had been practised against her; but she had taken their work from them, which was their only means to get

money, and was the same to them in the end. For instance—a
gentleman where she lived would give her a half dollar to hire
a poor man to clear the new-fallen snow from the steps and
sidewalks. She would arise early, and perform the labor herself,
putting the money into her own pocket. A poor man would
come along, saying she ought to have let him have the job; he
was poor, and needed the pay for his family. She would harden
her heart against him, and answer—"I am poor, too, and I need
it for mine." But, in her retrospection, she thought of all the
misery she might have been adding to, in her selfish grasping,
and it troubled her conscience sorely; and this insensibility to the
claims of human brotherhood, and the wants of the destitute and
wretched poor, she now saw, as she never had done before, to
be unfeeling, selfish, and wicked. These reflections and convic-
tions gave rise to a sudden revulsion of feeling in the heart of
Isabella, and she began to look upon money and property with
great indifference, if not contempt—being at that time unable,
probably, to discern any difference between a miserly grasping
at and hoarding of money and means, and a true use of the good
things of this life for one's own comfort, and the relief of such
as she might be enabled to befriend and assist. One thing she was
sure of—that the precepts, "Do unto others as ye would that
others should do unto you," "Love your neighbor as yourself,"
and so forth, were maxims that had been but little thought of by
herself, or practised by those about her.

Her next decision was, that she must leave the city; it was no
place for her; yea, she felt called in spirit to leave it, and to travel
east and lecture. She had never been further east than the city,
neither had she any friends there of whom she had particular
reason to expect any thing; yet to her it was plain that her
mission lay in the east, and that she would find friends there. She
determined on leaving; but these determinations and convic-
tions she kept close locked in her own breast, knowing that if her
children and friends were aware of it, they would make such an

ado about it as would render it very unpleasant, if not distressing
to all parties. Having made what preparations for leaving she
deemed necessary,—which was, to put a few articles of clothing
in a pillow-case, all else being deemed an unnecessary incum-
brance,—about an hour before she left, she informed Mrs.
Whiting, the woman of the house where she was stopping, that
her name was no longer Isabella, but SOJOURNER; and that she
was gong east. And to her inquiry, "What are you going east
for?" her answer was, "The Spirit calls me there, and I must go."

She left the city on the morning of the 1st of June, 1843,
crossing over to Brooklyn, L.I.; and taking the rising sun for her
only compass and guide, she "remembered Lot's wife," and
hoping to avoid her fate, she resolved not to look back till she
felt sure the wicked city from which she was fleeing was left too
far behind to be visible in the distance; and when she first
ventured to look back, she could just discern the blue cloud of
smoke that hung over it, and she thanked the Lord that she was
thus far removed from what seemed to *her* a second Sodom.

She was now fairly started on her pilgrimage; her bundle in
one hand, and a little basket of provisions in the other, and two
York shillings in her purse—her heart strong in the faith that her
true work lay before her, and that the Lord was her director; and
she doubted not he would provide for and protect her, and that
it would be very censurable in her to burden herself with any
thing more than a moderate supply for her then present needs.
Her mission was not merely to travel east, but to "lecture," as
she designated it; "testifying of the hope that was in her"—
exhorting the people to embrace Jesus, and refrain from sin, the
nature and origin of which she explained to them in accordance
with her own most curious and original views. Through her life,
and all its chequered changes, she has ever clung fast to her first
permanent impressions on religious subjects.

Wherever night overtook her, there she sought for lodgings—free, if she might—if not, she paid; at a tavern, if she

chanced to be at one—if not, at a private dwelling; with the rich, if they would receive her—if not, with the poor.

But she soon discovered that the largest houses were nearly always full; if not quite full, company was soon expected; and that it was much easier to find an unoccupied corner in a small house than in a large one; and if a person possessed but a miserable roof over his head, you might be sure of a welcome to part of it.

But this, she had penetration enough to see, was quite as much the effect of a want of sympathy as of benevolence; and this was also very apparent in her religious conversations with people who were strangers to her. She said, "she never could find out that the rich had any religion. If *I* had been rich and accomplished, I could; for the rich could always find religion in the rich, and *I* could find it among the poor."

At first, she attended such meetings as she heard of, in the vicinity of her travels, and spoke to the people as she found them assembled. Afterwards, she advertised meetings of her own, and held forth to large audiences, having, as she said, "a good time."

When she became weary of travelling, and wished a place to stop a while and rest herself, she said some opening for her was always near at hand; and the first time she needed rest, a man accosted her as she was walking, inquiring if she was looking for work. She told him that was not the object of her travels, but that she would willingly work a few days, if any one wanted. He requested her to go to his family, who were sadly in want of assistance, which he had been thus far unable to supply. She went to the house where she was directed, and was received by his family, one of whom was ill, as a "God-send"; and when she felt constrained to resume her journey, they were very sorry, and would fain have detained her longer; but as she urged the necessity of leaving, they offered her what seemed in her eyes a great deal of money as a remuneration for her labor, and an expression of their gratitude for her opportune assistance; but she would only receive a very little of it; enough, as she says, to enable her to pay tribute to Cæsar, if it was demanded of her; and two or three York shillings at a time were all she allowed herself to take; and then, with purse replenished, and strength renewed, she would once more set out to perform her mission.

THE CONSEQUENCES OF REFUSING A TRAVELLER A NIGHT'S LODGING

As she drew near the centre of the Island, she commenced, one evening at nightfall, to solicit the favor of a night's lodging. She had repeated her request a great many, it seemed to her some twenty times, and as many times she received a negative answer. She walked on, the stars and the tiny horns of the new-moon shed but a dim light on her lonely way, when she was familiarly accosted by two Indians, who took her for an acquaintance. She told them they were mistaken in the person; she was a stranger there, and asked them the direction to a tavern. They informed her it was yet a long way—some two miles or so; and inquired if she were alone. Not wishing for their protection, or knowing what might be the character of their kindness, she answered, "No, not exactly," and passed on. At the end of a weary way, she came to the tavern,—or, rather, to a large building, which was occupied as court-house, tavern, and jail,—and on asking for a night's lodging, was informed she could stay, if she would consent to be locked in. This to her mind was an insuperable objection. To have a key turned on her was a thing not to be thought of, at least not to be endured; and she again took up her line of march, preferring to walk beneath the open sky, to being locked up by a stranger in such a place. She had not walked far, before she heard the voice of a woman under an open shed; she ventured to accost her, and inquired if she knew where she could get in for the night. The woman answered, that she did not, unless she went home with them; and turning to her "good man," asked him if the stranger could not share their home for the night, to which he cheerfully assented. Sojourner thought it evident he had been taking a drop too much, but as he was civil and good-natured, and she did not feel inclined to spend the night alone in the open air, she felt driven to the necessity of accepting their hospitality, whatever it might prove to be. The woman soon informed her that there was a ball in the place, at which they would like to drop in a while, before they went to their home.

Balls being no part of Sojourner's mission, she was not desirous of attending; but her hostess could be satisfied with nothing short of a taste of it, and she was forced to go with her, or relinquish their company at once, in which move there might be more exposure than in accompanying her. She went, and soon found herself surrounded by an assemblage of people, collected from the very dregs of society, too ignorant and degraded to understand, much less entertain, a high or bright idea,—in a dirty hovel, destitute of every comfort, and where the fumes of whiskey were abundant and powerful.

Sojourner's guide there was too much charmed with the combined entertainments of the place to be able to tear herself away, till she found her faculties for enjoyment failing her, from a too free use of liquor; and she betook herself to bed till she could recover them. Sojourner, seated in a corner, had time for many reflections, and refrained from lecturing them, in obedience to the recommendation, "Cast not your pearls," &c. When the night was far spent, the husband of the sleeping woman aroused the sleeper, and reminded her that she was not very polite to the woman she had invited to sleep at her house, and of the propriety of returning home. They once more emerged into the pure air, which to our friend Sojourner, after so long breathing the noisome air of the ball-room, was most refreshing and grateful. Just as day dawned, they reached the place they called their home. Sojourner now saw that she had lost nothing in the shape of rest by remaining so long at the ball, as their miserable cabin afforded but one bunk or pallet for sleeping; and had there been many such, she would have preferred sitting up all night to occupying one like it. They very politely offered her the bed, if she would use it; but civilly declining, she waited for morning with an eagerness of desire she never felt before on the subject, and was never more happy than when the eye of day shed its golden light once more over the earth. She was once more free, and while daylight should last, independent, and needed no invitation to pursue her journey. Let these facts teach us, that every pedestrian in the world is not a vagabond, and that it is a dangerous thing to compel any one to receive that hospitality from the vicious and abandoned which they should have received from us,—as thousands can testify, who have thus been caught in the snares of the wicked.

The fourth of July, Isabella arrived at Huntingdon; from thence she went to Cold Springs, where she found the people making preparations for a mass temperance-meeting. With her usual alacrity, she entered into their labors, getting up dishes *a la New York,* greatly to the satisfaction of those she assisted. After remaining at Cold Springs some three weeks, she returned to Huntingdon, where she took boat for Connecticut. Landing at Bridgeport, she again resumed her travels towards the northeast, lecturing some, and working some, to get wherewith to pay tribute to Cæsar, as she called it; and in this manner she presently came to the city of New Haven, where she found many meetings, which she attended—at some of which, she was allowed to express her views freely, and without reservation. She also called meetings expressly to give herself an opportunity to be heard; and found in the city many true friends of Jesus, as she judged, with whom she held communion of spirit, having no preference

for one sect more than another, but being well satisfied with all
who gave her evidence of having known or loved the Savior.

After thus delivering her testimony in this pleasant city, feeling she had not as yet found an abiding place, she went from
thence to Bristol, at the request of a zealous sister, who desired
her to go to the latter place, and hold a religious conversation
with some friends of hers there. She went as requested, found
the people kindly and religiously disposed, and through them
she became acquainted with several very interesting persons.

A spiritually-minded brother in Bristol, becoming interested
in her new views and original opinions, requested as a favor that
she would go to Hartford, to see and converse with friends of his
there. Standing ready to perform any service in the Lord, she
went to Hartford as desired, bearing in her hand the following
note from this brother:—

"Sister,—I send you this living messenger, as I believe
her to be one that God loves. Ethiopia is stretching forth
her hands unto God. You can see by this sister, that God
does by his Spirit alone teach his own children things to
come. Please receive her, and she will tell you some new
things. Let her tell her story without interrupting her, and
give close attention, and you will see she has got the lever
of truth, that God helps her to pry where but few can. She
cannot read or write, but the law is in her heart.

"Send her to brother ———, brother ———, and
where she can do the most good.
                    "From your brother,
                    "H. L. B."

SOME OF HER VIEWS AND REASONINGS

❂

As soon as Isabella saw God as an all-powerful, all-pervading spirit, she became desirous of hearing all that had been written of him, and listened to the account of the creation of the world and its first inhabitants, as contained in the first chapters of Genesis, with peculiar interest. For some time she received it all literally, though it appeared strange to her that "God worked by the day, got tired, and stopped to rest," &c. But after a little time, she began to reason upon it, thus—"Why, if God works by the day, and one day's work tires him, and he is obliged to rest, either from weariness or on account of darkness, or if he waited for the 'cool of the day to walk in the garden,' because he was inconvenienced by the heat of the sun, why then it seems that God cannot do as much as *I* can; for *I* can bear the sun at noon, and work several days and nights in succession without being much tired. Or, if he rested nights because of the darkness, it is very queer that he should make the night so dark that he could not see himself. If *I* had been God, I would have made the night light enough for my own convenience, surely." But the moment she placed this idea of God by the side of the impression she had once so suddenly received of his inconceivable greatness and entire spirituality, that moment she exclaimed mentally, "No, God does not stop to rest, for he is a spirit, and cannot tire; he cannot want for light, for he hath all light in himself. And if 'God is all in all,' and 'worketh all in all,' as I have heard them read, then it is impossible he should rest at all; for if he did, every other thing would stop and rest too; the waters would not flow, and the fishes could not swim; and all motion must cease. God could have no pauses in his work, and he needed no Sabbaths of rest. Man might need them, and he should take them when he needed them, whenever he required rest. As it regarded the worship of God, he was to be worshipped at all times and in all places; and one portion of time never seemed to her more holy than another."

These views, which were the results of the workings of her own mind, assisted solely by the light of her own experience and very limited knowledge, were, for a long time after their adoption, closely locked in her own breast, fearing lest their avowal might bring upon her the imputation of "infidelity,"—the usual charge preferred by all religionists, against those who entertain religious views and feelings differing materially from their own. If, from their own sad experience, they are withheld from shouting the cry of "infidel," they fail not to see and to feel, ay, and to say, that the dissenters are not of the right spirit, and that their spiritual eyes have never been unsealed.

While travelling in Connecticut, she met a minister, with whom she held a long discussion on these points, as well as on various other topics, such as the origin of all things, especially the origin of evil, at the same time bearing her testimony strongly against a paid ministry. He belonged to that class, and, as a matter of course, as strongly advocated his own side of the question.

I had forgotten to mention, in its proper place, a very important fact, that when she was examining the scriptures, she wished to hear them without comment; but if she employed adult persons to read them to her, and she asked them to read a passage over again, they invariably commenced to explain, by giving her their version of it; and in this way, they tried her feelings exceedingly. In consequence of this, she ceased to ask adult persons to read the Bible to her, and substituted children in their stead. Children, as soon as they could read distinctly, would re-read the same sentence to her, as often as she wished, and without comment;—and in that way she was enabled to see what her own mind could make out of the record, and that, she said, was what she wanted, and not what others thought it to mean. She wished to compare the teachings of the Bible with the witness within her; and she came to the conclusion, that the spirit of truth spoke in those records, but that the recorders of those truths had intermingled with them ideas and suppositions of their own. This is one among the many proofs of her energy and independence of character.

When it became known to her children, that Sojourner had left New York, they were filled with wonder and alarm. Where could she have gone, and why had she left? were questions no one could answer satisfactorily. Now, their imaginations painted her as a wandering maniac—and again they feared she had been left to commit suicide; and many were the tears they shed at the loss of her.

But when she reached Berlin, Conn., she wrote to them by amanuensis, informing them of her whereabouts, and waiting an answer to her letter; thus quieting their fears, and gladdening their hearts once more with assurances of her continued life and her love.

THE SECOND ADVENT DOCTRINES

In Hartford and vicinity, she met with several persons who believed in the "Second Advent" doctrines; or, the immediate personal appearance of Jesus Christ. At first she thought she had never heard of "Second Advent." But when it was explained to her, she recollected having once attended Mr. Miller's meeting in New York, where she saw a great many enigmatical pictures hanging on the wall, which she could not understand, and which, being out of the reach of her understanding, failed to interest her. In this section of country, she attended two camp-meetings of the believers in these doctrines—the "second advent" excitement being then at its greatest height. The last meeting was at Windsor Lock. The people, as a matter of course, eagerly inquired of her concerning her belief, as it regarded their most important tenet. She told them it had not been revealed to her; perhaps, if she could read, she might see it differently. Sometimes, to their eager inquiry, "Oh, don't you believe the Lord is coming?" she answered, "I believe the Lord is as near as he can be, and not be it." With these evasive and non-exciting answers, she kept their minds calm as it respected her unbelief, till she could have an opportunity to hear their views fairly stated, in order to judge more understandingly of this matter, and see if, in her estimation, there was any good ground for expecting an event which was, in the minds of so many, as it were, shaking the very foundations of the universe. She was invited to join them in their religious exercises, and accepted the invitation—praying, and talking in her own peculiar style, and attracting many about her by her singing.

When she had convinced the people that she was a lover of God and his cause, and had gained a good standing with them, so that she could get a hearing among them, she had become quite sure in her own mind that they were laboring under a delusion, and she commenced to use her influence to calm the fears of the people, and pour oil upon the troubled waters. In one part of the grounds, she found a knot of people greatly excited: she mounted a stump and called out, "Hear! hear!" When the people had gathered around her, as they were in a state to listen to any thing new, she addressed them as "children," and asked them why they made such a "To-do;—are you not commanded to 'watch and pray?' You are neither watching nor praying." And she bade them, with the tones of a kind mother, retire to their tents, and there watch and pray, without noise or tumult, for the Lord would not come to such a scene of confusion; "the Lord came still and quiet." She assured them, "the Lord might come, move all through the camp, and go away again, and they never know it," in the state they then were.

They seemed glad to seize upon any reason for being less

agitated and distressed, and many of them suppressed their noisy terror, and retired to their tents to "watch and pray"; begging others to do the same, and listen to the advice of the good sister. She felt she had done some good, and then went to listen further to the preachers. They appeared to her to be doing their utmost to agitate and excite the people, who were already too much excited; and when she had listened till her feelings would let her listen silently no longer, she arose and addressed the preachers. The following are specimens of her speech:—

"Here you are talking about being 'changed in the twinkling of an eye.' If the Lord should come, he'd change you to *nothing*! for there is nothing to you.

"You seem to be expecting to go to some parlor *away up* somewhere, and when the wicked have been burnt, you are coming back to walk in triumph over their ashes—this is to be your New Jerusalem! ! Now, *I* can't see any thing so very *nice* in that, coming back to such a *muss* as that will be, a world covered with the ashes of the wicked! Besides, if the Lord comes and burns—as you say he will—I am not going away; *I* am going to stay here and *stand the fire,* like Shadrach, Meshach, and Abednego! And Jesus will walk with me through the fire, and keep me from harm. Nothing belonging to God can burn, any more than God himself; such shall have no need to go away to escape the fire! No, *I* shall remain. Do you tell me that God's children *can't stand fire*?" And her manner and tone spoke louder than words, saying, "It is *absurd* to think so!"

The ministers were taken quite aback at so unexpected an opposer, and one of them, in the kindest possible manner, commenced a discussion with her, by asking her questions, and quoting scripture to her; concluding, finally, that although she had learned nothing of the great doctrine which was so exclusively occupying their minds at the time, she had learned much that man had never taught her.

At this meeting, she received the address of different persons, residing in various places, with an invitation to visit them. She promised to go soon to Cabotville, and started, shaping her course for that place. She arrived at Springfield one evening at six o'clock, and immediately began to search for a lodging for the night. She walked from six till past nine, and was then on the road from Springfield to Cabotville, before she found any one sufficiently hospitable to give her a night's shelter under their roof. Then a man gave her twenty-five cents, and bade her go to a tavern and stay all night. She did so, returning in the morning to thank him, assuring him she had put his money to its legitimate use. She found a number of the friends she had seen at Windsor when she reached the manufacturing town of Ca-botville, (which has lately taken the name of Chicopee,) and with them she spent a pleasant week or more; after which, she left them to visit the Shaker village in Enfield. She now began to think of finding a resting place, at least, for a season; for she had performed quite a long journey, considering she had walked most of the way; and she had a mind to look in upon the Shakers, and see how things were there, and whether there was any opening there for her. But on her way back to Springfield, she called at a house and asked for a piece of bread; her request was granted, and she was kindly invited to tarry all night, as it was getting late, and she would not be able to stay at every house in that vicinity, which invitation she cheerfully accepted. When the man of the house came in, he recollected having seen her at the camp-meeting, and repeated some conversations, by which she recognized him again. He soon proposed having a meeting that evening, went out and notified his friends and neighbors, who came together, and she once more held forth to them in her peculiar style. Through the agency of this meeting, she became acquainted with several people residing in Springfield, to whose houses she was cordially invited, and with whom she spent some pleasant time.

One of these friends, writing of her arrival there, speaks as follows. After saying that she and her people belonged to that class of persons who believed in the second advent doctrines; and that this class, believing also in freedom of speech and action, often found at their meetings many singular people, who did not agree with them in their principal doctrine; and that, being thus prepared to hear new and strange things, "They listened eagerly to Sojourner, and drank in all she said";—and also, that she "soon became a favorite among them; that when she arose to speak in their assemblies, her commanding figure and dignified manner hushed every trifler into silence, and her singular and sometimes uncouth modes of expression never provoked a laugh, but often were the whole audience melted into tears by her touching stories." She also adds, "Many were the lessons of wisdom and faith I have delighted to learn from her." . . . "She continued a great favorite in our meetings, both on account of her remarkable gift in prayer, and still more remarkable talent for singing, . . . and the aptness and point of her remarks, frequently illustrated by figures the most original and expressive.

"As we were walking the other day, she said she had often thought what a beautiful world this would be, when we should see every thing right side up. Now, we see every thing topsy-turvy, and all is confusion." For a person who knows nothing of this fact in the science of optics, this seemed quite a remarkable idea.

"We also loved her for her sincere and ardent piety, her unwavering faith in God, and her contempt of what the world calls fashion, and what we call folly.

"She was in search of a quiet place, where a way-worn traveller might rest. She had heard of Fruitlands,[20] and was inclined to go there; but the friends she found here thought it best for her to visit Northampton. She passed her time, while with us, working wherever her work was needed, and talking where work was not needed.

"She would not receive money for her work, saying she

worked for the Lord; and if her wants were supplied, she received it as from the Lord.

"She remained with us till far into winter, when we introduced her at the Northampton Association." . . . "She wrote to me from thence, that she had found the quiet resting place she had so long desired. And she has remained there ever since."

ANOTHER CAMP-MEETING

When Sojourner had been at Northampton a few months, she attended another camp-meeting, at which she performed a very important part.

A party of wild young men, with no motive but that of entertaining themselves by annoying and injuring the feelings of others, had assembled at the meeting, hooting and yelling, and in various ways interrupting the services, and causing much disturbance. Those who had the charge of the meeting, having tried their persuasive powers in vain, grew impatient and tried threatening.

The young men, considering themselves insulted, collected their friends, to the number of a hundred or more, dispersed themselves through the grounds, making the most frightful noises, and threatening to fire the tents. It was said the authorities of the meeting sat in grave consultation, decided to have the ring-leaders arrested, and sent for the constable, to the great displeasure of some of the company, who were opposed to such an appeal to force and arms. Be that as it may, Sojourner, seeing great consternation depicted in every countenance, caught the contagion, and, ere she was aware, found herself quaking with fear.

Under the impulse of this sudden emotion, she fled to the most retired corner of a tent, and secreted herself behind a trunk, saying to herself, "I am the only colored person here, and on me, probably, their wicked mischief will fall first, and perhaps fatally." But feeling how great was her insecurity even there, as the very tent began to shake from its foundations, she began to soliloquise as follows:—

"Shall I run away and hide from the Devil? Me, a servant of the living God? Have I not faith enough to go out and quell that mob, when I know it is written—'One shall chase a thousand, and two put ten thousand to flight'? I know there are not a thousand here; and I know I am a servant of the living God. I'll go to the rescue, and the Lord shall go with and protect me.

"Oh," said she, "I felt as if I had *three hearts!* and that they were so large, my body could hardly hold them!"

She now came forth from her hiding-place, and invited several to go with her and see what they could do to still the raging of the moral elements. They declined, and considered her wild to think of it.

The meeting was in the open fields—the full moon shed its saddened light over all—and the woman who was that evening to address them was trembling on the preachers' stand. The noise and confusion were now terrific. Sojourner left the tent alone and unaided, and walking some thirty rods to the top of a small rise of ground, commenced to sing, in her most fervid manner, with all the strength of her most powerful voice, the hymn on the resurrection of Christ—

It was early in the morning—it was early in the morning,
   Just at the break of day—
When he rose—when he rose—when he rose,
   And went to heaven on a cloud.

All who have ever heard her sing this hymn will probably remember it as long as they remember her. The hymn, the tune, the style, are each too closely associated with to be easily separated from herself, and when sung in one of her most animated moods, in the open air, with the utmost strength of her most powerful voice, must have been truly thrilling.

As she commenced to sing, the young men made a rush towards her, and she was immediately encircled by a dense body of the rioters, many of them armed with sticks or clubs as their weapons of defence, if not of attack. As the circle narrowed around her, she ceased singing, and after a short pause, inquired, in a gentle but firm tone, "Why do you come about me with clubs and sticks? I am not doing harm to any one." "We ar'n't a going to hurt you, old woman; we came to hear you sing," cried many voices, simultaneously. "Sing to us, old woman," cries one. "Talk to us, old woman," says another. "Pray, old woman," says a third. "Tell us your experience," says a fourth. "You stand and smoke so near me, I cannot sing or talk," she answered.

"Stand back," said several authoritative voices, with not the most gentle or courteous accompaniments, raising their rude weapons in the air. The crowd suddenly gave back, the circle became larger, as many voices again called for singing, talking, or praying, backed by assurances that no one should be allowed to hurt her—the speakers declaring with an oath, that they would *"knock down"* any person who should offer her the least indignity.

She looked about her, and with her usual discrimination, said inwardly—"Here must be many young men in all this assemblage, bearing within them hearts susceptible of good impressions. I will speak to them." She did speak; they silently heard, and civilly asked her many questions. It seemed to her to be given her at the time to answer them with truth and wisdom beyond herself. Her speech had operated on the roused passions of the mob like oil on agitated waters; they were, as a whole, entirely subdued, and only clamored when she ceased to speak or sing. Those who stood in the back ground, after the circle was

enlarged, cried out, "Sing aloud, old woman, we can't hear."
Those who held the sceptre of power among them requested
that she should make a pulpit of a neighboring wagon. She said,
"If I do, they'll overthrow it." "No, they sha'n't—he who dares
hurt you, we'll knock him down instantly, d——n him," cried
the chiefs. "No we won't, no we won't, nobody shall hurt you,"
answered the many voices of the mob. They kindly assisted her
to mount the wagon, from which she spoke and sung to them
about an hour. Of all she said to them on the occasion, she
remembers only the following:—

"Well, there are two congregations on this ground. It is
written that there shall be a separation, and the sheep shall be
separated from the goats. The other preachers have the sheep,
I have the goats. And I have a few sheep among my goats, but
they are *very* ragged." This exordium produced great laughter.
When she became wearied with talking, she began to cast about
her to contrive some way to induce them to disperse. While she
paused, they loudly clamored for "more," "more,"—"sing,"
"sing more." She motioned them to be quiet, and called out to
them: "Children, I have talked and sung to you, as you asked
me; and now I have a request to make of you; will you grant it?"
"Yes, yes, yes," resounded from every quarter. "Well, it is this,"
she answered; "if I will sing one more hymn for you, will you
then go away, and leave us this night in peace?" "Yes, yes,"
came faintly, feebly from a few. "I repeat it," says Sojourner,
"and I want an answer from you all, as of one accord. If I will
sing you one more, will you go away, and leave us this night in
peace?" "Yes, yes, yes," shouted many voices, with hearty emphasis. "I repeat my request once more," said she, "and I want
you *all* to answer." And she reiterated the words again. This time
a long, loud "Yes—yes—yes," came up, as from the multitudi-
nous mouth of the entire mob. "AMEN! it is SEALED," repeated
Sojourner, in the deepest and most solemn tones of her powerful
and sonorous voice. Its effect ran through the multitude, like an

electric shock; and the most of them considered themselves bound by their promise, as they might have failed to do under less imposing circumstances. Some of them began instantly to leave; others said, "Are we not to have one more hymn?" "Yes," answered their entertainer, and she commenced to sing:

> I bless the Lord I've got my seal—to-day and to-day—
> To slay Goliath in the field—to-day and to-day;
> The good old way is a righteous way,
> I mean to take the kingdom in the good old way.

While singing, she heard some enforcing obedience to their promise, while a few seemed refusing to abide by it. But before she had quite concluded, she saw them turn from her, and in the course of a few minutes, they were running as fast as they well could in a solid body; and she says she can compare them to nothing but a swarm of bees, so dense was their phalanx, so straight their course, so hurried their march. As they passed with a rush very near the stand of the other preachers, the hearts of the people were smitten with fear, thinking that their entertainer had failed to enchain them longer with her spell, and that they were coming upon them with redoubled and remorseless fury. But they found they were mistaken, and that their fears were groundless; for, before they could well recover from their surprise, every rioter was gone, and not one was left on the grounds, or seen there again during the meeting. Sojourner was informed that as her audience reached the main road, some distance from the tents, a few of the rebellious spirits refused to go on, and proposed returning; but their leaders said, "No—we have promised to leave—all promised, and we must go, all go, and you shall none of you return again."

She did not fall in love at first sight with the Northampton Association, for she arrived there at a time when appearances did not correspond with the ideas of associationists, as they had been spread out in their writings; for their phalanx was a factory, and they were wanting in means to carry out their ideas of beauty and elegance, as they would have done in different circumstances. But she thought she would make an effort to tarry with them one night, though that seemed to her no desirable affair. But as soon as she saw that accomplished, literary, and refined persons were living in that plain and simple manner, and submitting to the labors and privations incident to such an infant institution, she said, "Well, if these can live here, *I* can." Afterwards, she gradually became pleased with, and attached to, the place and the people, as well she might; for it must have been no small thing to have found a home in a "Community composed of some of the choicest spirits of the age," where all was characterized by an equality of feeling, a liberty of thought and speech, and a largeness of soul, she could not have before met with, to the same extent, in any of her wanderings.

Our first knowledge of her was derived from a friend who had resided for a time in the "Community," and who, after describing her, and singing one of her hymns, wished that we might see her. But we little thought, at that time, that we should ever pen these "simple annals" of this child of nature.

When we first saw her, she was working with a hearty good will; saying she would not be induced to take regular wages, believing, as once before, that now Providence had provided her with a never-failing fount, from which her every want might be perpetually supplied through her mortal life. In this, she had calculated too fast. For the Associationists found, that, taking every thing into consideration, they would find it most expedient to act individually; and again, the subject of this sketch found her dreams unreal, and herself flung back upon her own resources for the supply of her needs. This she might have found more inconvenient at her time of life—for labor, exposure, and hardship had made sad inroads upon her iron constitution, by inducing chronic disease and premature old age—had she not remained under the shadow of one,* who never wearies in doing good, giving to the needy, and supplying the wants of the destitute. She has now set her heart upon having a little home of her own, even at this late hour of life, where she may feel a greater freedom than she can in the house of another, and where she can repose a little, after her day of action has passed by. And for such a "home" she is now dependant on the charities of the benevolent, and to them we appeal with confidence.

Through all the scenes of her eventful life may be traced the energy of a naturally powerful mind—the fearlessness and child-like simplicity of one untrammelled by education or conventional customs—purity of character—an unflinching adherence to principle—and a native enthusiasm, which, under different circumstances, might easily have produced another Joan of Arc.

With all her fervor, and enthusiasm, and speculation, her religion is not tinctured in the least with gloom. No doubt, no hesitation, no despondency, spreads a cloud over her soul; but all is bright, clear, positive, and at times ecstatic. Her trust is in God, and from him she looks for good, and not evil. She feels that "perfect love casteth out fear."

Having more than once found herself awaking from a mortifying delusion,—as in the case of the Sing-Sing kingdom,—and resolving not to be thus deluded again, she has set suspicion to guard the door of her heart, and allows it perhaps to be aroused by too slight causes, on certain subjects—her vivid imagination assisting to magnify the phantoms of her fears into gigantic proportions, much beyond their real size; instead of resolutely adhering to the rule we all like best, when it is to be applied to ourselves—that of placing every thing we see to the account of the best possible motive, until time and circumstance prove that

*George W. Benson.

we were wrong. Where no good motive can be assigned, it may
become our duty to suspend our judgment till evidence can be
had.

In the application of this rule, it is an undoubted duty to
exercise a commendable prudence, by refusing to repose any
important trust to the keeping of persons who may be strangers
to us, and whose trustworthiness we have never seen tried. But
no possible good, but incalculable evil may and does arise from
the too common practice of placing all conduct, the source of
which we do not fully understand, to the worst of intentions.
How often is the gentle, timid soul discouraged, and driven
perhaps to despondency, by finding its "good evil spoken of";
and a well-meant but mistaken action loaded with an evil design!

If the world would but sedulously set about reforming itself
on this one point, who can calculate the change it would pro-
duce—the evil it would annihilate, and the happiness it would
confer! None but an all-seeing eye could at once embrace so vast
a result. A result, how desirable! and one that can be brought
about only by the most simple process—that of every individual
seeing to it that he commit not this sin himself. For why should
we allow in ourselves, the very fault we most dislike, when
committed against us? Shall we not at least aim at consistency?

Had she possessed less generous self-sacrifice, more knowledge of the world and of business matters in general, and had she
failed to take it for granted that others were like herself, and
would, when her turn came to need, do as she had done, and
find it "more blessed to give than to receive," she might have
laid by something for the future. For few, perhaps, have ever
possessed the power and inclination, in the same degree, at one
and the same time, to labor as she has done, both day and night,
for so long a period of time. And had these energies been
well-directed, and the proceeds well husbanded, since she has
been her own mistress, they would have given her an independence during her natural life. But her constitutional biases, and

her early training, or rather want of training, prevented this result; and it is too late now to remedy the great mistake. Shall she then be left to want? Who will not answer, "No!"

LAST INTERVIEW WITH HER MASTER

In the spring of 1849, Sojourner made a visit to her eldest daughter, Diana, who has ever suffered from ill health, and remained with Mr. Dumont, Isabella's humane master. She found him still living, though advanced in age, and reduced in property, (as he had been for a number of years,) but greatly enlightened on the subject of slavery. He said he could then see that "slavery was the wickedest thing in the world, the greatest curse the earth had ever felt—that it was then very clear to his mind that it was so, though, while he was a slaveholder himself, he did not see it so, and thought it was as right as holding any other property." Sojourner remarked to him, that it might be the same with those who are now slaveholders. "Oh, no," replied he, with warmth, "it cannot be. For, now, the sin of slavery is so clearly written out, and so much talked against,— (why, the whole world cries out against it!)—that if any one says he don't know, and has not heard, he must, I think, be a liar. In my slaveholding days, there were few that spoke against it, and these few made little impression on any one. Had it been as it is now, think you I could have held slaves? No! I should not have dared to do it, but should have emancipated every one of them. Now, it is very different; all may hear if they will."

Yes, reader, if any one feels that the tocsin of alarm, or the anti-slavery trump, must sound a louder note before they can hear it, one would think they must be very hard of hearing,— yea, that they belong to that class, of whom it may be truly said, "they have stopped their ears that they may not hear."

She received a letter from her daughter Diana, dated Hyde Park, December 19, 1849, which informed her that Mr. Dumont had "gone West" with some of his sons—that he had taken along with him, probably through mistake, the few articles of furniture she had left with him. "Never mind," says Sojourner, "what we give to the poor, we lend to the Lord." She thanked the Lord with fervor, that she had lived to hear her master say such blessed things! She recalled the lectures he used to give his slaves, on speaking the truth and being honest, and laughing, she says he taught us not to lie and steal, when *he* was stealing all the time himself, and did not know it! Oh! how sweet to my mind was this confession! And what a confession for a master to make to a slave! A slaveholding master turned to a brother! Poor old man, may the Lord bless him, and all slaveholders partake of his spirit!

END OF THE NARRATIVE

CERTIFICATES OF CHARACTER

HURLEY, ULSTER CO., Oct. 13th, 1834

This is to certify, that I am well acquainted with Isabella, this colored woman; I have been acquainted with her from her infancy; she has been in my employ for one year, and she was a faithful servant, honest, and industrious; and have always known her to be in good report by all who employed her.

ISAAC S. VAN WAGENEN

NEW PALTZ, ULSTER CO., Oct. 13th, 1834

This is to certify, that Isabella, this colored woman, lived with me since the year 1810, and that she has always been a good and faithful servant; and the eighteen years that she was with me, I always found her to be perfectly honest. I have always heard her well spoken of by every one that has employed her.

JOHN J. DUMONT

NORTHAMPTON, March, 1850

We, the undersigned, having known Isabella (or Sojourner Truth) for several years, most cheerfully bear testimony to her uniform good character, her untiring industry, kind deportment, unwearied benevolence, and the many social and excellent traits which make her worthy to bear her adopted name.

GEO. W. BENSON

S. L. HILL

A. W. THAYER[21]

BOSTON, March, 1850

My acquaintance with the subject of the accompanying Narrative, Sojourner Truth, for several years past, has led me to form a very high appreciation of her understanding, moral integrity, disinterested kindness, and religious sincerity and enlightenment. Any assistance or co-operation that she may receive in the sale of her Narrative, or in any other manner, I am sure will be meritoriously bestowed.

WM. LLOYD GARRISON

Notes

INTRODUCTION

✦

[1] *Battle Creek Journal,* December 5, 1883; *The Liberator,* October 12, 1850; Olive Gilbert, *Narrative of Sojourner Truth, A Northern Slave, Emancipated from Bodily Servitude by the State of New York in 1828, including a Book of Life,* ed. by Frances Titus (New York, 1878), 168; Walter M. Merrill and Louis Ruchames, eds. *The Letters of William Lloyd Garrison* (Cambridge, Mass. 1981), 6:536.

[2] The Tercentenary History Committee, *The Northampton Book: Chapters from 300 Years in the Life of a New England Town, 1654–1954* (Northampton, Mass., 1954), 345–82; Frederick Douglass, "What I Found at the Northampton Association," Charles A. Sheffield, ed., *The History of Florence, Massachusetts, Including a Complete Account of the Northampton Association of Education and Industry* (Florence, Mass., 1895), 132.

[3] Gilbert, *Narrative and Book of Life,* 140–43.

[4] Harriet Beecher Stowe, "Sojourner Truth, the Libyan Sibyl." *Atlantic Monthly,* (April 1863), 473.

[5] Sojourner Truth to Mary Gale, February 23, 1864; Sojourner Truth to Diana Corbin, November 3, 1864; Elizabeth Leggett to Amy Post, 186?, all in Isaac and Amy Post Family Papers (hereafter IAPFP), University of Rochester; Sojourner Truth to *The National Anti-Slavery Standard,* December 17, 1864; Gilbert, *Narrative and Book of Life,* 140–43, 183–99.

[6] Sojourner Truth to Amy Post, October 1, 1865; Laura S. Haviland to Amy Post, February 22, 1866; P. Glennan to Sojourner Truth, March 25, 1867; G. W. Weeks to Sojourner Truth, March 21, 1867; all in IAPFP; *Narrative and Book of Life*, 183–99.

[7] Sojourner Truth to Mary Gayle, April 15, 1853, Manuscripts Division, Library of Congress; Diary of Henry Chandler, 1857–58, Minnie Merritt Fay Collection, Michigan Historical Collections, Bentley Historical Library, University of Michigan.

[8] Josephine Griffing to Sojourner Truth, January 7, 1867; Sojourner Truth to Amy Post, January 18, 1869; Esther Titus to Amy Post, n.d.; Laura Haviland to Amy Post, February 22, 1866; Cora Daniels to Amy Post, February 16, 1827; Phebe Merritt to Sojourner Truth, April 17, 1867; all in IAPFP; Recollections of Minnie Merritt Fay, Kemball House Historical Museum, Battle Creek, Mich.

[9] Josephine J. Franklin to Mrs. Sojourner Truth, May 31, 1864, Leggett Family Manuscripts—Scrapbook, Michigan Historical Collections, Bentley Historical Library (originals in Detroit Public Library).

[10] The 1817 law freed outright all slaves born before 1799 as of July 4, 1827. Those born after July 4, 1799, served until the ages of twenty-five, if female, and twenty-eight, if male. Arthur Zilversmit, *The First Emancipation: The Abolition of Slavery in the North* (Chicago, 1967), 213–14; A. Leon Higginbotham, *In the Matter of Color: Race and the American Legal Process, The Colonial Period* (New York, 1978), 143–44.

[11] Sylvester Judd Notebook, October 20, 1845, Judd Manuscripts, Forbes Library, Northampton, Mass.; Gilbert, *Narrative and Book of Life*, 146–47.

[12] Edgar J. McManus, *Black Bondage in the North* (Syracuse, 1973), 2–4, 11, 59–60; James A. Rawley, *The Transatlantic Slave Trade* (New York and London, 1981), 88–90; Joyce D. Goodfriend, "Burghers and Blacks: The Evolution of a Slave Society at New Amsterdam," *New York History*, 59 (1978): 124–44; Graham R. Hodges, "Root and Branch: The Black Experience in Colonial New York and New Jersey," forthcoming, ch. 1.

[13] Zilversmit, *First Emancipation;* McManus, *Black Bondage,* ch. 5; Thomas J. Davis, "New York's Long Black Line: A Note on the Growing Slave Population, 1626–1790" in *Afro-Americans in New York Life and History* (January, 1978), 44, 48–49; South Carolina's gelding punishment was for runaways. In both cases, the Lords of Trade denounced such "inhumane" penalties, and the Privy Council disallowed the law.

[14] McManus refers to Curaçao Africans as "assimilated" (*Black Bondage,* 8); Rawley, *Slave Trade,* 88, 92–96, 385–89; Joseph C. Miller, *Way of Death: Merchant Capitalism and the Angolan Slave Trade, 1730–1830* (Madison, 1988), 142–43; Hodges, "Root and Branch," 30–43.

[15] This myth has been published for years. As late as 1989, Joanne M. Braxton in her otherwise excellent though brief discussion of Sojourner Truth referred to Isabella as "African-born." See Braxton, *Black Women Writing Autobiography: A Tradition Within a Tradition* (Philadelphia, 1989), 74.

[16] McManus, *Black Bondage,* 209–12; Davis, "New York's Long Black Line," 41–59.

[17] John S. Ezell, ed. *The New Democracy in America: Travels of Francisco de Miranda;* trans. by Judson Wood-Pittier (Caracas, 1987), 99; Myrtle Hardenbergh Miller, *The Hardenbergh Family: A Genaeological Compilation* (New York, 1958), 26–30; Evers, *The Catskills: From Wilderness to Woodstock* (Garden City, N.Y., 1972), 33–39, 46–52, Mederic-Louis-Elie Moreau de Saint-Mery, *Moreau de St. Mery's American Journey, 1793–1798,* trans. by Kenneth Roberts and Anna M. Roberts (Garden City, N.Y., 1947), 272; David Steven Cohen, *The Dutch-American Farm* (New York, 1992); Shane White, *Somewhat More Independent: The End of Slavery in New York City, 1770–1810,* (Athens, Ga., 1991), 59–62, ch. 4.

[18] White, *Somewhat More Independent,* ch. 4, Zilversmit, *First Emancipation,* 29–32; A. J. Williams-Myers, "Masters and Slaves in the Hudson River Valley." *Afro-Americans in New York Life and History:* III (March 1985); Hodges, "Root and Branch," chs. 2–4.

[19] George Pratt, "An Account of the British Expedition." *Ulster County Historical Society Collections,* 1 (Kingston, 1860), 120, 142; E. B. O'Callaghan, *The Documentary History of the State of New York* (Albany, 1850), 969, 970; Miller, *Hardenbergh Family,* 29, 31, 53–56, 58–61, 62, 75; Evers, *Catskills,* 252.

[20] McManus, *Black Bondage;* Williams-Meyers, "Masters and Slaves," 94–96; Hodges, "Root and Branch," ch. 6–7; White, *Somewhat More Independent,* 18–21, ch. 4.

[21] Gary B. Nash and Jean R. Soderlund, *Freedom by Degrees: Emancipation in Pennsylvania and Its Aftermath* (New York, 1991), esp. ch. 4; Hodges, "Root and Branch," ch. 6–7; White, *Somewhat More Independent,* 18–21, ch. 4.

[22] Zilversmit, *First Emancipation,* 151, 160, 182.

[23] Ibid., 160, 176–79, 180–83.

[24] Ulster County Wills, Bk. C, No. 164; Bk. D, No. 196; Williams-Myers, "Masters and Slaves," 86; Barbara Jean Fields, *Slavery on the Middle Ground* (New Haven, 1987), 25–27.

[25] A 1785 bill allowed masters to free a slave without posting the 200-pound bond if overseers of the poor stipulated that the slave was under fifty years old and capable of taking care of herself or himself. Zilversmit, *First Emancipation,* 148.

[26] Ibid., 213–14.

[27] Clifford Geertz, *Interpretation of Cultures* (New York, 1973), 89.

[28] Vivienne L. Kruger, "Born to Run: The Slave Family in Early New York, 1626–1827," Ph.D. dissertation (Columbia University, 1985); White, *Somewhat More Independent,* 89–95, 113; Zilversmit, *First Emancipation,* 9–11.

[29] Sojourner bought a house in Northampton, Massachusetts, which she sold to move permanently to the utopian village of Harmonia,

outside Battle Creek, Michigan, in 1857. Several years later, a schism at Harmonia prompted her to leave, although she retained the property. After a time, she bought property in Battle Creek, which was her home base until she died. All of her children and their families moved to be with her, some remaining at Harmonia, others residing in Battle Creek.

[30] Francis X. Weiser, *Handbook of Christian Feasts and Customs: The Year of the Lord in Liturgy and Folklore* (New York, 1970), 246–55; Cohen, *Dutch-American Farm*, 161–63, 180; A. J. Williams-Myers, "Pinkster Carnival: Africanisms in the Hudson River Valley," *Afro-Americans in New York Life and History*, 9 (January 1985), 7–17; Hodges, "Root and Branch," ch. 7.

[31] Williams-Myers, "Pinkster Carnival," 9. Clearly the Pan-African component of Pinkster-like holidays has been demonstrated. For examples outside New York, see William Pierson, *Black Yankees: The Development of an Afro-American Subculture in Eighteenth Century New England* (Amherst, Mass., 1988), ch. 10. See also: Sterling Stuckey, *Nationalist Theory and the Foundations of Black America* (New York, 1987); Hodges, "Root and Branch," ch. 7; Robert Farris Thompson and Joseph Cornet, *The Four Moments of the Sun: Kongo Art in Two Worlds* (Washington, 1981), 27; White, *Somewhat More Independent*, ch. 4. White disagrees with the assessment that an African cultural presence exists in the Pinkster festival.

[32] Charles T. Davis and Henry Louis Gates, Jr., eds. *The Slave's Narrative* (New York, 1985), xxiv–xxvii. See also Henry Louis Gates, Jr., *The Signifying Monkey: A Theory of African-American Literary Criticism* (New York, 1988), ch. 4.

[33] Davis and Gates, *Slave's Narrative*, xxix–xxxi.

[34] Graham R. Hodges, *Black Resistance in Colonial and Revolutionary Bergen County, New Jersey* (River Edge, N.J.), 10–11; Robert Farris Thompson, *Flash of the Spirit: African and Afro-American Art and Philosophy* (New York, 1983), 103–142; Thompson and Cornet, *Four Moments of the Sun*, 194–95; "Black Burial Ground Revealing Glimpses of the Past," *The New York Times*, August 9, 1992, p. 45.

[35] Dominique Zahan, *The Religion, Spirituality, and Thought of Traditional Africa,* trans. by Kate Ezra and Lawrence M. Martin (Chicago and London, 1970), 126–30.

[36] Barbara Welter, "The Cult of True Womanhood, 1820–1860." *American Quarterly* 18 (Summer, 1966), 151–174; Hazel V. Carby, *Reconstruction Womanhood: The Emergence of the Afro-American Woman Novelist* (New York, 1987), ch. 2. For alternate perspectives on "the cult of true womanhood," see Elizabeth Fox-Genovese, *Within the Plantation Household: Black and White Women of the Old South* (Chapel Hill, 1988), esp. ch. 4. The author refutes the idea that Southern and Northern women had identical ideas, standards, and customs about the role of women.

[37] Jean Fagan Yellin, *Women and Sisters: The Antislavery Feminists in American Culture* (New Haven, 1989), 125–50; Melton A. McLaurin, *Celia, A Slave: A True Story of Violence and Retribution in Antebellum Missouri* (Athens, Ga., 1991). This work is excellent documentation of white attitudes toward morality among slaves, although it offers no insights into the female slave's perspective. Carby, *Reconstruction Womanhood,* ch. 2; Deborah Gray White, *Ar'n't I A Woman: Female Slaves in the Plantation South* (New York, 1985), ch. 1, and 152–53, 164, 165.

[38] Harriet A. Jacobs, *Incidents in the Life of a Slave Girl, Written by Herself,* ed. Lydia Maria Child (Boston, 1861), annotated and edited by Jean Fagan Yellin (Cambridge, Mass., 1987), 3–4. Yellin, *Women and Sisters,* 87. Yellin considers Sojourner's *Narrative* a secondary source and her speech *("Ar'n't I A Woman")* primary information (p. 198). On this point we disagree. The *Narrative* was in fact dictated by Sojourner, and her speech, which Yellin considers primary material, was written years later by Frances Gage, as she remembered it. Gage's version does not correspond with the accounts of Sojourner's Akron, Ohio, speech written at the time in antislavery newspapers (see, for example the *Anti-Slavery Bugle,* June 21, 1851, in the Appendix to this volume). Not only is Gage's version self-serving in tone, but she misrepresents Sojourner by quoting her in strong Southern dialect (a device also used by Stowe in the *Atlantic Monthly*). Stowe's article was also recollection written ten years after their meeting in 1853.

[39] Gilbert, *Narrative and Book of Life*, 138–39; Harryette Mullen, "Indelicate Subjects": African-American Women's Subjugated Subjectivity." *Sub/Versions: Feminist Studies Works in Progress* (University of California, Santa Cruz), Winter 1991, 1–7.

[40] Jacobs, *Incidents in the Life of a Slave Girl*, 3–4.

THE NARRATIVE

❂

[1] The year 1797 seems correct. Isabella was emancipated under the 1817 law, which freed all blacks (at age twenty-five if female, twenty-eight if male) in New York born before July 4, 1799, as of July 4, 1827. Also, when John Dumont purchased her in 1810, he was told that she was between twelve and fourteen. See Arthur Zilversmit, *The First Emancipation: The Abolition of Slavery in the North* (Chicago, 1967), 213–14. See also Dumont's letter in Gilbert Vale, *Fanaticism: Its Source and Influence, Illustrated by the Simple Narrative of Isabella in the Case of Matthias, Mr. and Mrs. B. Folger, Mr. Pierson, Mr. Mills, Catharine, Isabella, &c. &c.* (New York, 1835), 11.

[2] This was Johannes Hardenbergh, of Swartekill, Esopus. See Myrtle Hardenbergh Miller, *The Hardenbergh Family: A Genealogical Compilation* (New York, 1958), 53–59, 60–62, 74–75. See also *New York Heads of Families at the First Census of the United States Taken in the Year 1790* (Baltimore, 1966), 170. Isabella's first owner, Colonel Johannes Hardenbergh, born in 1729, is listed in the 1790 census as having seven slaves. His will is dated October 26, 1799. He is missing from the census, taken in 1800, when he would have been about seventy-one years old. But his son, Charles, not listed in 1790, is listed in the 1800 census as owning six slaves. This corroborates Sojourner's memory that her family passed to Charles Hardenbergh (also a colonel) after the death of her first master. U.S. Bureau of the Census, *Second Census, 1800* (Washington, D.C., 1801), 208.

[3] If born in 1797, Isabella was eleven or twelve when the sale occurred, rather than nine. Charles Hardenbergh died in 1808. Isabella, her parents, and her brother are listed in the inventory of Hardenbergh's estate. Charles' will provided that all of his real estate and chattle be sold (Ulster County wills, Book D, 196–98).

[4] Olive Gilbert could easily have determined when Isabella's mother died. Isabella certainly could tell seasons and knew who her owner was at the time of her mother's death. If Bett lived several years, Isabella undoubtedly was about fifteen or sixteen when Bett died, and was at the Dumonts'.

[5] The correct spelling is Neely. Isabella and Dumont's information corroborate that she lived with the Neelys in 1808. Also, instead of a slave category, the 1810 census has "Persons except Indians not taxed." John Neely had no one in this category. Dumont had three. See U.S. Bureau of the Census, Third Census (Washington, D.C., 1811), 745, 713; H. Hendricks, "Sojourner Truth: Her Early History in Slavery," National Magazine 16 (1892), 668.

[6] The correct spelling is Schriver, sometimes spelled Schryver. Martinus Schryver kept a saloon in Kingston. See U.S. Bureau of the Census, First Census (Washington, D.C., 1791), 172; U.S. Bureau of the Census, Third Census, 743; Marius Schoonmacher, The History of Kingston, New York, From Its Early Settlement to the Year 1820 (New York, 1888); Hendricks, "Sojourner Truth," 666.

[7] The date should be July 4, 1827. See Zilversmit, First Emancipation, 213–14.

[8] Isabella's known children were Diana, Peter, Elizabeth, and Sophia. Diana was the eldest and Peter probably the second eldest. Both were born before 1820. Elizabeth was most likely born in 1822 and Sophia in 1826. Some accounts state that Isabella had another son named James, who died in infancy. Others indicate that a fourth daughter named Hannah or Nancy existed (although Hannah could have been a nickname for Diana). At least two accounts state that Diana was not born on the Dumont farm. In the City Directory (1869–70), her age is listed as 56, placing her birth around 1813. On the Burial Record at

Oak Hill Cemetery in Battle Creek, Michigan, Diana's age is listed as "100," an obvious error, since she died in 1904 (suggesting that Isabella bore her at the age of seven). U.S. Bureau of the Census, *Fourth Census* (Washington, D.C., 1821), 71; U.S. Bureau of the Census, *Fifth Census* (Washington, D.C., 1831), 203; Hendricks, "Sojourner Truth," 669; *Three Rivers Tribune,* November 4, 1904; *Battle Creek Journal,* October 25, 1904; Battle Creek, Michigan, City Directories, 1869–70.

[9] The correct spelling is Van Wagenen. See Certificates of Character, p. 103.

[10] The correct spelling is Gidney; see U.S. Bureau of the Census, *Sixth Census* (Washington, D.C., 1841), 32–33. Solomon Gidney had one slave in 1840. His brother, Eleazer Gidney, was a practicing dentist in England. See Joseph Gidney Papers, Rare Book Room, New York Public Library.

[11] See note 1.

[12] Charles W. Chipp, called Squire Chipp, was an attorney who was elected county clerk. He never practiced law. See Nathaniel Sylvester, *History of Ulster County* (Kingston, 1880), 106; Charles Howard Burnett, *The Chipp Family in England and America* (Los Angeles, 1933), 136–40.

[13] This would have been one of the Romeyn brothers (Herman M. and John T.). Both attorneys came to Ulster County in 1823. Herman M. was the better known. Sylvester, *Ulster County,* 103; *Ulster Plebian,* December 16, 1820.

[14] The circuit court judge in the case was the Honorable Charles H. Ruggles of Poughkeepsie. Ruggles also officiated in New York in 1834 at the Matthias trial in which Isabella was implicated, but from which she was exonerated. Sylvester, *Ulster County,* 154; Henry Stoddard Ruggles, *The Ruggles Family in England and America* (Privately printed, 1896), 157; Gilbert Vale, *Fanaticism: Its Source and Influence, Illustrated by the Simple Narrative of Isabella in the Case of Matthias, Mr. and Mrs. B. Folger, Mr. Pierson, Mr. Mills, Catharine, Isabella, &c. &c.* (New York: 1835), 114.

[15] Pinkster.

[16] The law took effect July 4, 1827.

[17] The name of the ship was *Zone*. See Sidney Kaplan's article in *Negro History Bulletin* (November 1955).

[18] Here is a reference to a sister, "Hannah," who may have been Diana. Isabella's known adult daughters were Diana, Elizabeth, and Sophia.

[19] Nancy may have been the name given to Isabella's sister by her white masters, while Dinah was the name given her by Mau-mau Bett.

[20] Fruitlands was a utopian community established by Bronson Alcott in 1843 in the town of Harvard, forty miles from Boston. Like Brook Farm, Fruitlands was a Transcendentalist community where "simplicity and order" were guiding principles and where people of "superior cultivation" lived modestly and creatively. See Clara Endicott Sears, ed., *Bronson Alcott's Fruitlands* (Boston, 1915), ch. 1–2.

[21] Benson, Hill, and Thayer were founders of Northampton. Benson was the brother-in-law of William Lloyd Garrison.

Appendices

SOJOURNER TRUTH'S "AR'N'T I A WOMAN" SPEECH

WILLIAM LLOYD GARRISON'S PREFACE
TO THE 1850 EDITION

Sojourner Truth's
"Ar'n't I a Woman" Speech

✿

AN IMAGE of Sojourner Truth made popular by activist Frances Gage was her address at the 1851 Women's Rights Convention in Akron, Ohio. Years later, Gage remembered that the tall, gaunt, and Quaker-attired Sojourner Truth cowed a disruptive, unruly crowd by her practical eloquence and persuasive powers. She reportedly saved the day for the women's cause with her "A'rn't I a Woman?" oration. The veracity of Gage's recall of Sojourner's speech is questionable. But the *Anti-Slavery Bugle*'s on-the-scene account is more accurate than Gage's. Here is Sojourner's famous address as it was recorded rather than as it was remembered:

One of the most unique and interesting speeches of the Convention was made by Sojourner Truth, an emancipated slave. It is impossible to transfer it to paper, or convey any adequate idea of the effect it produced upon the audience. Those only can appreciate it who saw her powerful form, her whole-souled, earnest gesture, and listened to her strong and truthful tones. She came forward to the platform and addressing the President said with great simplicity: "May I say a few words?" Receiving an affirmative answer, she proceeded:

I want to say a few words about this matter. I am a woman's rights. I have as much muscle as any man, and can do as much work as any man. I have plowed and reaped and husked and chopped and mowed, and can any man do more than that? I have heard much about the sexes being equal. I can carry as much as any man, and can eat as much too, if I can get it. I am as strong as any man that is now. As for intellect, all I can say is, if woman have a pint, and man a quart—why can't she have her little pint full? You need not be afraid to give us our rights for fear we will take too much,—for we can't take more than our pint'll hold. The poor men seem to be all in confusion, and don't know what to do. Why children, if you have woman's rights, give it to her and you will feel better. You will have your own rights, and they won't be so much trouble. I can't read, but I can hear. I have heard the bible and have learned that Eve caused man to sin. Well, if woman upset the world, do give her a chance to set it right side up again. The Lady has spoken about Jesus, how he never spurned woman from him, and she was right. When Lazarus died, Mary and Martha came to him with faith and love and besought him to raise their brother. And Jesus wept and Lazarus came forth. And how came Jesus into the world? Through God who created him and a woman who bore him. Man, where is your part? But the women are coming up blessed be God and a few of the men are coming up with them. But man is in a tight place, the poor slave is on him, woman is coming on him, he is surely between a hawk and a buzzard.

Anti-Slavery Bugle, June 21, 1851

William Lloyd Garrison's Preface
to the 1850 Edition

✿

THE FOLLOWING is the unpretending narrative of the life of a remarkable and meritorious woman—a life which has been checkered by strange vicissitudes, severe hardships, and singular adventures. Born a slave, and held in that brutal condition until the entire abolition of slavery in the State of New York in 1827, she has known what it is to drink to the dregs the bitterest cup of human degradation. That one thus placed on a level with cattle and swine, and for so many years subjected to the most demoralizing influences, should have retained her moral integrity to such an extent, and cherished so successfully the religious sentiment of her soul, shows a mind of no common order, while it heightens the detestation that is felt in every humane bosom, of that system of oppression which seeks to cripple the intellect, impair the understanding, and deprave the hearts of its victims—a system which has subjected to its own foul purposes, in the United States, all that is wealthy, talented, influential, and reputedly pious, in an overwhelming measure!

O the "fantastic tricks" which the American people are "playing before high Heaven"! O their profane use of the sacred name of Liberty! O their impious appeals to the God of the oppressed, for his divine benediction, while they are making merchandise of his image! Do they not blush? Nay, they glory in their shame! Once a year, they take special pains to exhibit themselves to the world, in all their republican deformity and Christian barbarity, insanely supposing that they thus excite the envy, admiration, and applause of mankind. The nations are looking at the dreadful spectacle with disgust and amazement. However sunken and degraded they may be, they are too elevated, too virtuous, too humane to be guilty of such conduct. Their voice is heard, saying—"Americans! we hear your boasts of liberty, your shouts of independence, your declarations of hostility to every form of tyranny, your assertions that all men are created free and equal, and endowed by their Creator with an inalienable right to liberty, the merry peal of your bells, and the deafening roar of your artillery; but, mingling with all these, and rising above them all, we also hear the clanking of chains! the shrieks and wailings of millions of your own countrymen, whom you wickedly hold in a state of slavery as much more frightful than the oppression which your fathers resisted unto blood, as the tortures of the Inquisition surpass the stings of an insect! We see your banner floating proudly in the breeze from every flag-staff and mast-head in the land; but its blood-red stripes are emblematical of your own slave-driving cruelty, as you apply the lash to the flesh of your guiltless victim, even the flesh of a wife and mother, shrieking for the restoration of the babe of her bosom, sold to the remorseless slave speculator! We catch the gleam of your illuminated hills, every where blazing with bonfires; we mark your gay processions; we note the number of your orators; we listen to the recital of your revolutionary achievements; we see you kneeling at the shrine of Freedom, as her best, her truest, her sincerest worshippers! Hypocrites! liars! adulterers! tyrants! men-stealers! atheists! Professing to believe in the natural equality of the human race—yet dooming a sixth portion of your immense population to beastly servitude, and ranking them among your goods and chattels! Professing to believe in the existence of a God—yet trading in his image, and selling those in the shambles for whose redemption the Son of God laid down his life! Professing to be Christians—yet withholding the Bible, the means of religious instruction, even the knowledge of the alphabet, from a benighted multitude, under terrible penalties! Boasting of your democracy—yet determining the rights of men by the texture of their hair and the color of their skin! Assuming to be "the land of the free and the home of the brave,—yet keeping in chains more slaves than any other nation, not excepting slave-cursed Brazil! Prating of your morality and honesty—yet denying the rites of marriage to three millions of human beings, and plundering them of all their hard earnings! Affecting to be horror-struck in view of the foreign slave-trade—yet eagerly pursuing a domestic traffic equally cruel and unnatural, and reducing to slavery not less than seventy thousand new victims annually! Vaunting of your freedom of speech and of the press—your matchless Constitution and your glorious Union—yet denouncing as traitors, and treating as outlaws, those who have the courage and fidelity to plead for immediate, untrammelled, universal emancipation! Monsters that ye are! how can ye expect to escape the scorn of the world, and the wrath of Heaven? Emancipate your slaves, if you would redeem your tarnished character—if you would obtain forgiveness here, and salvation hereafter! Until you do so, 'there will be a stain upon your national escutcheon, which all the waters of the Atlantic cannot wash out!' "

It is thus that, as a people, we are justly subjected to the reproach, the execration, the derision of mankind, and are made a proverb and a hissing among the nations. We cannot plead not guilty; every accusation that is registered against us is true; the act of violence is in our hands; the stolen property is in our possession; our fingers are stained with blood; the cup of our iniquity is full.

Just God! and shall we calmly rest,
     The Christian's scorn—the Heathen's mirth—
Content to live the lingering jest
     And by-word of a mocking earth?
Shall our own glorious land retain
     That curse which Europe scorns to bear?
Shall our own brethren drag the chain,
     Which not even Russia's menials wear?

It is useless, it is dreadful, it is impious for this nation longer to contend with the Almighty. All his attributes are against us, and on the side of the oppressed. Is it not a fearful thing to fall into the hands of the living God? Who may abide the day of his coming, and who shall stand when he appeareth as "a swift witness against the adulterers, and against false swearers, and against those who oppress the hireling in his wages, the widow, and the fatherless, and that turn aside the stranger from his right?" Wo to this bloody land! it is all full of lies and robbery—the prey departeth not, and the sound of a whip is heard continually. "Judgment is turned away backward, and justice standeth afar off; for truth is fallen in the street, and equity cannot enter. Yea, truth faileth; and he that departeth from evil, *maketh himself a prey.*" The Lord sees it, and is displeased that there is no judgment; and he hath put on the garments of vengeance for clothing, and is clad with zeal as a cloak,—and unless we repent by immediately undoing the heavy burdens and letting the oppressed go free, according to our deeds, accordingly he will repay, fury to his adversaries, recompense to his enemies. "The Lord executeth righteousness and judgment for all that are oppressed." "O give thanks unto the Lord; for he is good: for his mercy endureth for ever. To him that smote Egypt in their first-born: for his mercy endureth for ever. And overthrew Pharaoh and his hosts in the Red sea; for his mercy endureth for ever." "Sing unto the Lord, for he hath triumphed gloriously:

the horse and his rider hath he thrown into the sea. Thou didst blow with thy wind, the sea covered them: they sank as lead in the mighty waters." "Even so, Lord God Almighty, for so it seemeth good in thy sight." "Who is like unto thee, O Lord, among the gods? who is like thee, glorious in holiness, fearful in praises, doing wonders?"

In this great contest of Right against Wrong, of Liberty against Slavery, who are the wicked, if they be not those, who, like vultures and vampyres, are gorging themselves with human blood? if they be not the plunderers of the poor, the spoilers of the defenceless, the traffickers in "slaves and the souls of men"? Who are the cowards, if not those who shrink from manly argumentation, the light of truth, the concussion of mind, and a fair field? if not those whose prowess, stimulated by whiskey potations, or the spirit of murder, grows rampant as the darkness of night approaches; whose shouts and yells are savage and fiend-like; who furiously exclaim, "Down with free discussion! down with the liberty of the press! down with the right of petition! down with constitutional law!"—who rifle mail-bags, throw types and printing-presses into the river, burn public halls dedicated to "Virtue, Liberty and Independence," and assassinate the defenders of inalienable human rights? And who are the righteous, in this case, if they be not those who will "have no fellowship with the unfruitful works of darkness, but rather reprove them"; who maintain that the laborer is worthy of his hire, that the marriage institution is sacred, that slavery is a system accursed of God, that tyrants are the enemies of mankind, and that immediate emancipation should be given to all who are pining in bondage! Who are the truly brave, if not those who demand for truth and error alike, free speech, a free press, an open arena, the right of petition, AND NO QUARTERS? if not those, who, instead of skulking from the light, stand forth in the noon-tide blaze of day, and challenge their opponents to emerge from their wolf-like dens, that, by a rigid examination, it may be seen who has stolen the wedge of gold, in whose pocket are the thirty pieces of silver, and whose garments are stained with the blood of innocence?

It is hoped that the perusal of the following Narrative may increase the sympathy that is felt for the suffering colored population of this country, and inspire to renewed efforts for the liberation of all who are pining in bondage on the American soil.

Note on Editions of
Sojourner Truth's Narrative

※

THE TEXT of the *Narrative of Sojourner Truth* reprinted here was first published in 1850, simultaneously in Boston and New York. The amanuensis was Olive Gilbert of Brooklyn, Connecticut. The *Narrative* included a preface by William Lloyd Garrison and an appendix, consisting of excerpts from Theodore Weld's *Slavery As It Is*. Perhaps as proof of authenticity, the last pages of the *Narrative* are statements entitled "Certificates of Character," from Northampton and Ulster County. Dr. James Boyle, Sojourner's Northampton friend and neighbor, financed publication of the *Narrative*. In 1855, it was reprinted with a brief introduction by Harriet Beecher Stowe.

In 1875, Boyle gave Sojourner, then a Michigan resident, the stereotype plates of her *Narrative* as a gift. With the help of Frances Titus, her friend in Battle Creek, Sojourner published later editions of the *Narrative* in 1875, 1878, and 1881. These included a *"Book of Life."* Compiled by Titus, this "book" consisted of tributary correspondence and testimonials from longtime friends, selections from newspapers, and autographs of notable reformers and politicians. In 1884, one year after Sojourner's death, the *Narrative* and *"Book of Life"* were again reprinted, with an additional memorial chapter.

Like most nineteenth-century slave narratives, Sojourner Truth's was not subsequently reprinted until the civil rights movement ushered in a persistent call for African-American history. In 1968, Arno Press reprinted the 1878 edition of the *Narrative and "Book of Life."* That edition is no longer in print. In 1992, Oxford University Press published the *Narrative and Book of Life* as part of the Arthur Schomberg Collection, with a brief, literary introduction by Professor Jeffrey Stewart.

The present edition of the original 1850 *Narrative of Sojourner Truth* is the only printing containing a substantial historical introduction. The purpose of this introduction is to illuminate some of the major features and contextual significance of the *Narrative,* and to encourage a fuller appreciation of this important historical figure. My research on Sojourner Truth, in preparation for writing a biography, has convinced me of the *Narrative's* authenticity. Furthermore, Sojourner repeated from memory scenes and situations in the *Narrative* often enough over the years to substantiate its credibility. As amanuensis, Olive Gilbert undoubtedly took some liberties. She also employed the traditional literary techniques typical of antislavery narratives and nineteenth-century sentimental writing. Certain exclusions, occasional lengthy dialogues, and direct appeals to white readers seem to have been Gilbert's major liberties.

The historical impact of Sojourner Truth begins with her slave narrative. Had she not tasted the bitter fruits of bondage, she might have remained an unknown nineteenth-century black woman. But slavery gave voice to Sojourner Truth, and she championed veracity as strongly as she defended the causes of her race and gender.

Except for occasional changes in punctuation, nothing in this reproduction of the 1850 *Narrative* has been altered. However, occasional notes have been added to identify people, provide correct spellings of names, and offer additional clarifying information. (These notes are numbered; all others that appear in the text were printed in the 1850 edition.) My sources for these annotations were census records, wills, published works, and manuscript information.

Bibliography

Most SECONDARY MATERIAL about Sojourner Truth contains many distortions, which makes compiling a bibliography a difficult and selective endeavor. What follows in the category of secondary sources is a carefully considered group of materials, either scholarly works or accounts that corroborate firsthand information specifically related to Sojourner Truth. Using such standards limits selection but ensures some reliability in separating reality from the myths surrounding the persona of Sojourner Truth.

Searches for primary material lead to greater success, as I discovered in research for her biography. Wherever she went, Sojourner's impact was felt and noted by many people and presses. Diaries, reminiscences, letters, journal articles, individual collections, and newspapers yield a wealth of information about this unschooled black leader. Moreover, Sojourner's dictated correspondence provides insights and access to her life and times. Thus, the attentive historian can trace the checkered footsteps of this fascinating woman's walk through history. A sample of the primary literature is included here.

Several undocumented, nonscholarly books on the life of Sojourner Truth have been published and are noted in the last section of this bibliography. The authors are not professional historians, and they took creative liberties that are important in telling a good story but sometimes vary from fact. Nevertheless, these books offer the casual reader a sense of the significance of Sojourner Truth.

SECONDARY SOURCES

Bliven, Bruce, and Helen Collins. *A Mirror for Greatness: Six Americans.* New York, 1975.

Collins, Kathleen. "Shadow and Substance: Sojourner Truth." *History of Photography* 7, 3 (July–September 1983).

Hendricks, H. "Sojourner Truth: Her Early History in Slavery." *National Magazine* 16 (1892).

Mabee, Carleton. "Sojourner Truth and President Lincoln." *New England Quarterly* 61 (December 1990).

———. "Sojourner Truth, Bold Prophet: Why Did She Never Learn to Read?" *New York History* 69 (January 1988).

———. "Sojourner Truth Fights Dependence on Government: Moves Freed Slaves off Welfare in Washington to Jobs in Upstate New York." *Afro-Americans in New York Life and History* 14, 1 (January 1990).

McBee, Alice Eaton. *From Utopia to Florence, the Story of Transcendentalist Community in Northampton, Mass.* Menasha, Wis., 1947.

McDade, Thomas. "Matthias, Prophet without Honor." *New-York Historical Society Quarterly* 63, 3 (July 1978).

Mullen, Harryette. " 'Indelicate Subjects': African-American Women's Subjugated Subjectivity," *Sub/Versions: Feminist Studies Works in Progress* [University of California, Santa Cruz], Winter 1991.

Painter, Nell I. "Sojourner Truth in Life and Memory: Writing the Biography of an American Exotic." *Gender and History* 2, 1 (Spring 1990).

Shafer, Elizabeth. "Sojourner Truth: "A Self-made Woman." *American History Illustrated* 8, 9 (January 1974).

Yellin, Jean Fagan. *Women and Sisters: The Antislavery Feminists in American Culture*. New Haven, 1989.

PUBLISHED PRIMARY MATERIALS

Lowenberg, Bert, and Ruth Bogin, eds. *Black Women in Nineteenth-century American Life: Their Words, Their Thoughts, Their Feelings*. University Park, Md. 1977.

Matthews, Margaret. *Matthias, by His Wife: With Notes on the Book of Mr. Stone on Matthias*. New York, 1835.

Matthews, Robert. *Memoirs of Matthias the Prophet*. New York, 1835.

Porter, Dorothy. "Sojourner Truth Calls upon the President: An 1864 Letter," *Massachusetts Review* 13, 5 (1972).

Ripley, Peter C., ed. *The Black Abolitionist Papers*, 5 vols. Chapel Hill, 1987–1992.

Sheffield, Charles A., ed. *The History of Florence, Massachusetts, Including a Complete Account of the Northampton Association of Education and Industry.* Florence, Mass., 1895.

Sterling, Dorothy, ed. *Speak Out in Thunder Tones: Letters and Other Writings by Black Northerners, 1787–1865.* Garden City, N.Y., 1973.

———. *We Are Your Sisters: Black Women in the Nineteenth Century.* New York, 1984.

Stone, William Leete. *Matthias and His Imposters: or, The Progress of Fanaticism, Illustrated in the Extraordinary Case of Robert Matthews and Some of His Forerunners and Disciples.* New York, 1835.

˙Vale, Gilbert. *Fanaticism: Its Source and Influence, Illustrated by the Simple Narrative of Isabella in the Case of Matthias, Mr. and Mrs. B. Folger, Mr. Pierson, Mr. Mills, Catharine, Isabella, &c. &c., A Reply to W. L. Stone.* New York, 1835.

COLLECTIONS OF PRIMARY SOURCES

❖

Burton Historical Collection, Detroit Public Library, Detroit, Mich.

Bernice Lowe Collection, Bentley Historical Library, University of Michigan, Ann Arbor.

Isaac and Amy Post Family Papers, Rush Rhees Library, University of Rochester, Rochester, N.Y.

Sophia Smith Collection, Smith College, Northampton, Mass.

Sojourner Truth Collection, Library of Congress, Washington, D.C.

Willard Public Library, Battle Creek, Mich.

BOOKS ON SOJOURNER TRUTH

Bernard, Jacqueline. *Journey Toward Freedom: The Story of Sojourner Truth.* New York, 1967.

Fauset, Arthur H. *Sojourner Truth: God's Faithful Pilgrim.* Chapel Hill, 1938.

Ortiz, Victoria. *Sojourner Truth, a Self-made Woman.* New York, 1989.

Pauli, Hertha. *Her Name Was Sojourner Truth.* New York, 1962.

Index

About the Editor

Margaret Washington is Associate Professor of History at Cornell University. Her research and published work focus on African-American culture and on African-American women. She is the author of *A Peculiar People: Slave Religion and Community-Culture Among the Gullahs.* Professor Washington is currently writing a biography of the life and times of Sojourner Truth.

___ **The Ink Dark Moon: Love Poems** $10.00   0-679-72958-5
    by Ono No Komachi and Izumi Shikibu,
    Women of the Ancient Court of Japan,
      translated by Jane Hirshfield with Mariko Aratani

___ **The Panther and the Lash** by Langston Hughes $10.00   0-679-73659-X

___ **Selected Poems of Langston Hughes** $10.00   0-679-72818-X
    by Langston Hughes

___ **The Ways of White Folks** by Langston Hughes $9.00   0-679-72817-1

___ **Stories** by Katherine Mansfield, $12.00   0-679-73374-4
    with an introduction by Jeffrey Meyers

___ **The Republic of Plato**, translated by B. Jowett $9.00   0-679-73387-6

___ **Cyrano de Bergerac** by Edmond Rostand, $9.95   0-679-73413-9
    translated by Anthony Burgess

___ **The Tale of Genji** by Murasaki Shikibu, $11.00   0-679-72953-4
    translated and abridged by Edward Seidensticker

___ **Dr. Jekyll and Mr. Hyde** by Robert Louis Stevenson, $7.00   0-679-73476-7
    with an introduction by Joyce Carol Oates

___ **Democracy in America: Volume I** $12.00   0-679-72825-2
    by Alexis de Tocqueville,
    translated by Phillips Bradley,
    with an introduction by Daniel J. Boorstin

___ **Democracy in America: Volume II** $12.00   0-679-72826-0
    by Alexis de Tocqueville,
    translated by Phillips Bradley

___ **Narrative of Sojourner Truth** $9.00   0-679-74035-X
    by Sojourner Truth,
    edited and with an introduction by
    Margaret Washington

___ **Germinal** by Émile Zola $8.00   0-679-75430-X